HEBREWS

BOOKS OF FAITH SERIES
Leader Session Guide

Janet M. Corpus

HEBREWS
Leader Session Guide

Books of Faith Series
Book of Faith Adult Bible Studies

Copyright © 2010 Augsburg Fortress. All rights reserved. Except for brief quotations in critical articles or reviews, no part of this book may be reproduced in any manner without prior written permission from the publisher. For more information, visit: www.augsburgfortress.org/copyrights or write to: Permissions, Augsburg Fortress, Box 1209, Minneapolis, MN 55440-1209.

 Book of Faith is an initiative of the
Evangelical Lutheran Church in America
God's work. Our hands.

For more information about the Book of Faith initiative, go to www.bookoffaith.org.

Scripture quotations, unless otherwise marked, are from New Revised Standard Version Bible, copyright © 1989 Division of Christian Education of the National Council of Churches of Christ in the United States of America. Used by permission. All rights reserved.

Web site addresses are provided in this resource for your use. These listings do not represent an endorsement of the sites by Augsburg Fortress, nor do we vouch for their content for the life of this resource.

ISBN: 978-0-8066-9782-6
Writer: Janet M. Corpus
Cover and interior design: Spunk Design Machine, spkdm.com
Typesetting: PerfecType, Nashville, TN

The paper used in this publication meets the minimum requirements of American National Standard for Information Sciences—Permanence of Paper for Printed Library Materials, ANSI Z329.48-1984.

Manufactured in the U.S.A.
14 13 12 11 10 1 2 3 4 5 6 7 8 9 10

CONTENTS

	Introduction	5
1	Who Is Jesus? (Part 1) *Hebrews 1:1-14*	9
2	Who Is Jesus? (Part 2) *Hebrews 2:5-18*	19
3	What Did Jesus Do? *Hebrews 4:14—5:10; 9:24—10:1; 10:10-18*	27
4	What Is Faith? *Hebrews 11:1-40*	37
5	How Shall We Live? *Hebrews 12:1-17; 13:1-19*	47
6	What If Faith Fails? *Hebrews 4:12-13; 5:11—6:12; 10:19-29*	57

Introduction

Book of Faith Adult Bible Studies

Welcome to the conversation! The Bible study resources you are using are created to support the bold vision of the Book of Faith initiative that calls "the whole church to become more fluent in the first language of faith, the language of Scripture, in order that we might live into our calling as a people renewed, enlivened, empowered, and sent by the Word."

Simply put, this initiative and these resources invite you to "Open Scripture. Join the Conversation."

We enter into this conversation based on the promise that exploring the Bible deeply with others opens us to God working in and through us. God's Word is life changing, church changing, and world changing. Lutheran approaches to Scripture provide a fruitful foundation for connecting Bible, life, and faith.

A Session Overview

Each session is divided into the following four key sections. The amount of time spent in each section may vary based on choices you make. The core Learner Session Guide is designed for 50 minutes. A session can be expanded to as much as 90 minutes by using the Bonus Activities that appear in the Leader Session Guide.

- **Gather (10-15 minutes)**

Time to check in, make introductions, review homework assignments, share an opening prayer, and use the Focus Activity to introduce learners to the Session Focus.

- **Open Scripture (10-15 minutes)**

The session Scripture text is read using a variety of methods and activities. Learners are asked to respond to a few general questions. As leader, you may want to capture initial thoughts or questions on paper for later review.

- **Join the Conversation (25-55 minutes)**

Learners explore the session Scripture text through core questions and activities that cover each of the four perspectives (see diagram on p. 6). The core Learner Session Guide material may be expanded through use of the Bonus Activities provided in the Leader Session Guide. Each session ends with a brief Wrap-Up and prayer.

- **Extending the Conversation (5 minutes)**

Lists homework assignments, including next week's session Scripture text. The leader may choose one or more items to assign for all. Each session also includes additional Enrichment options and may include For Further Reading suggestions.

A Method to Guide the Conversation

Book of Faith Adult Bible Studies has three primary goals:

- To increase biblical fluency;
- To encourage and facilitate informed small group conversation based on God's Word; and
- To renew and empower us to carry out God's mission for the sake of the world.

To accomplish these goals, each session will explore one or more primary Bible texts from four different angles and contexts—historical, literary, Lutheran, and devotional. These particular ways of exploring a text are not new, but used in combination they provide a full understanding of and experience with the text.

Complementing this approach is a commitment to engaging participants in active, learner-orientated Bible conversations. The resources call for prepared leaders to facilitate learner discovery, discussion, and activity. Active learning and frequent engagement with Scripture will lead to greater biblical fluency and encourage active faith.

1 We begin by reading the Bible text and reflecting on its meaning. We ask questions and identify items that are unclear. We bring our unique background and experience to the Bible, and the Bible meets us where we are.

5 We return to where we started, but now we have explored and experienced the Bible text from four different dimensions. We are ready to move into the "for" dimension. We have opened Scripture and joined in conversation for a purpose. We consider the meaning of the text for faithful living. We wonder what God is calling us (individually and as communities of faith) to do. We consider how God's Word is calling us to do God's work in the world.

2* We seek to understand the world of the Bible and locate the setting of the text. We explore who may have written the text and why. We seek to understand the particular social and cultural contexts that influenced the content and the message. We wonder who the original audience may have been. We think about how these things "translate" to our world today.

Devotional Context

Historical Context

Lutheran Context

Literary Context

4 We consider the Lutheran principles that help ground our interpretation of the Bible text. We ask questions that bring those principles and unique Lutheran theological insights into conversation with the text. We discover how our Lutheran insights can ground and focus our understanding and shape our faithful response to the text.

3* We pay close attention to how the text is written. We notice what kind of literature it is and how this type of literature may function or may be used. We look at the characters, the story line, and the themes. We compare and contrast these with our own understanding and experience of life. In this interchange, we discover meaning.

* Sessions may begin with either Historical Context or Literary Context.

The diagram on p. 6 summarizes the general way this method is intended to work. A more detailed introduction to the method used in Book of Faith Adult Bible Studies is available in *Opening the Book of Faith* (Augsburg Fortress, 2008).

The Learner Session Guide

The Learner Session Guide content is built on the four sections (see p. 5). The content included in the main "Join the Conversation" section is considered to be the core material needed to explore the session Scripture text. Each session includes a Focus Image that is used as part of an activity or question somewhere within the core session. Other visuals (maps, charts, photographs, and illustrations) may be included to help enhance the learner's experience with the text and its key concepts.

The Leader Session Guide

For easy reference, the Leader Session Guide contains all the content included in the Learner Session Guide and more. The elements that are unique to the Leader Session Guide are the following:

- **Before You Begin**—Helpful tips to use as you prepare to lead the session.
- **Session Overview**—Contains detailed description of key themes and content covered in each of the four contexts (Historical, Literary, Lutheran, Devotional). Core questions and activities in the Learner Session Guide are intended to emerge directly from this Session Overview. Highlighted parts of the Session Overview provide a kind of "quick prep" for those wanting to do an initial scan of the key session themes and content.
- **Key Definitions**—Key terms or concepts that appear in the Session Overview may be illustrated or defined.
- **Facilitator's Prayer**—To help the leader center on the session theme and leadership task.
- **Bonus Activities**—Optional activities included in each of the four sections of "Join the Conversation" used by the leader to expand the core session.
- **Tips**—A variety of helpful hints, instructions, or background content to aid leadership facilitation.
- **Looking Ahead**—Reminders to the leader about preparation for the upcoming session.

Leader and Learner

In Book of Faith Adult Bible Studies, the leader's primary task is facilitating small group conversation and activity. These conversations are built around structured learning tasks. What is a structured learning task? It is an open question or activity that engages learners with new content and the resources they need to respond. Underlying this structured dialog approach are three primary assumptions about adult learners:

- Adult learners bring with them varied experiences and the capability to do active learning tasks;
- Adult learners learn best when they are invited to be actively involved in learning; and
- Adults are more accountable and engaged when active learning tasks are used.

Simply put, the goal is fluency in the first language of faith, the language of Scripture. How does one become fluent in a new language, proficient in building houses, or skilled at hitting a baseball? By practicing and doing in a hands-on way. Book of Faith Adult Bible Studies provides the kind of hands-on Bible exploration that will produce Bible-fluent learners equipped to do God's work in the world.

Books of Faith Series

Book of Faith Adult Bible Studies includes several series and courses. This Hebrews unit is part of the Books of Faith Series, which is designed to explore key themes and texts in the books of the Bible. Each book of the Bible reveals a unique story or message of faith. Many core themes and story lines and characters are shared by several books, but each book in its own right is a book of faith. Exploring these books of faith in depth opens us to the variety and richness of God's written word for us.

Hebrews Unit Overview

The book of Hebrews is a letter to second- or third-generation Christians, most of whom were likely raised in the faith from childhood. Their faith is flagging—perhaps they are distracted or taking their faith for granted. The writer is passionately concerned for their well-being. The letter to them is a sustained argument for the importance of faithfulness.

For the writer of Hebrews, the reason to be faithful is the person and work of Jesus Christ. Jesus—fully human and fully divine—accomplished what no other person and no other human work or ritual could. Jesus fulfilled God's plan of salvation. In his life, suffering, death, and resurrection, Jesus made God's plan and its fulfillment visible to us.

Speaking to people of a particular time and place—a Jewish Christian audience raised and living amid Hellenistic culture—the book draws on Hebrew scriptures and ritual traditions, as well as Greek philosophy.

Session 1 (Hebrews 1:1-14) asks, "Who Is Jesus? (Part 1)." The person Jesus Christ, Son of God, is fully divine, God's very being. In Jesus, God is visible. In Jesus, we know God directly. Jesus is superior to angels.

Session 2 (Hebrews 2:5-18) asks again, "Who Is Jesus? (Part 2)." To know Jesus fully is to know that Jesus is fully divine and fully human. Jesus is in every way like us—flesh and blood, able to suffer and die. Jesus became lower than angels.

Session 3 (Hebrews 4:14—5:10; 9:24—10:1; 10:10-18) asks, "What Did Jesus Do?" Jesus was obedient—he heard God's word and lived it, perfecting faith and fulfilling God's plan for our salvation. Because of who Jesus is—human and divine—Jesus healed the separation between heaven and earth. As high priest, he is served in both earth and heaven, historically and eternally.

Session 4 (Hebrews 11:1-40) asks, "What Is Faith?" Faith is hearing God's word with our whole lives—obeying God's promises in hopeful and expectant trust, despite appearances. As believers, we are preceded by a long line of the faithful who heard and acted on God's promises. They lived on the basis of God's promises, without yet seeing them realized.

Session 5 (Hebrews 12:1-17; 13:1-19) asks, "How Shall We Live?" Faith is active. It is a basis for living, a way of life. Jesus pioneered this way of life. Like athletes, we grow and are strengthened in faith through practice.

Session 6 (Hebrews 4:12-13; 5:11—6:12; 10:19-29) asks, "What If Faith Fails?" The original audience of Hebrews was becoming distracted and neglecting faith. The writer wanted both to uphold the people in faith and warn them, lest their salvation be at risk. When faith fails, we rely not only on faith *in* Jesus, but also on the faith *of* Jesus. Jesus' perfect love and perfect faith fulfill ours.

SESSION ONE

Hebrews 1:1-14

Leader Session Guide

Focus Statement

The person Jesus Christ, Son of God, is fully divine, God's very being. In Jesus, we see and know God.

Key Verse

He is the reflection of God's glory and the exact imprint of God's very being, and he sustains all things by his powerful word. When he had made purification for sins, he sat down at the right hand of the Majesty on high.
Hebrews 1:3

Focus Image

The Ascension, Giotto di Bondone / Arena Chapel, Cappella degli Scrovegni, Padua. © SuperStock/SuperStock

Who Is Jesus? (Part 1)

Session Preparation

Before You Begin . . .

Reflect on the session question: Who is Jesus? How have you experienced Jesus as God? What difference has that experience made in your life? How has that experience shaped or affected your faith? What words would you use to describe Jesus as divine? On a spectrum, do you relate to Jesus more as divine or as human?

Session Instructions

1. Read this Session Guide completely and highlight or underline any portions you wish to emphasize with the group. Note any Bonus Activities you wish to do.

2. If you plan to do any special activities, check to see what materials you'll need, if any.

4. Have extra Bibles on hand in case a member of the group forgets to bring one.

5. Have on hand copies of *Lutheran Book of Worship* and *Evangelical Lutheran Worship*. You may want to arrange for someone to play the piano or for some of the stronger singers in the group to be prepared to lead the singing.

Session Overview

The opening verses of Hebrews make emphatic assertions about the Son—Jesus—being God. This is central to the message of Hebrews. Learners may wonder about the apparent one-sidedness of these opening statements. Hebrews argues just as powerfully that Jesus is fully human. This session focuses on Jesus as divine, the next on Jesus as human.

SESSION ONE

Historical Context

Hebrews is one of the latest books of the Bible, written sometime between 60 and 100 C.E., approximately 30 to 70 years after Jesus' death. The author was highly educated and skilled in Greek, using the most eloquent Greek in the New Testament. The rhetorical style and theology are not those of the apostle Paul. Paul met the risen Christ on the road to Damascus (Acts 9:1-22); Hebrews' author heard of Christ from others (2:3).

The author was familiar both with Hebrew scripture and tradition and with Greek philosophical thought. Frequent references to Hebrew scripture and ritual practice suggest that the audience, too, was familiar with these traditions. Some in the original audience were probably second- or even third-generation followers of Jesus Christ. Perhaps because they were raised in the faith from childhood, they were taking their faith for granted and neglecting it. They may have faced a hostile environment and were growing weary of being faithful. Hebrews is a sustained argument for the importance of faithfulness.

The conversation of which Hebrews is a part is a conversation *within* a community of Jewish Christians. Some learners will be appropriately sensitive to passages that argue aspects of Christian belief or teaching as superseding aspects of Jewish belief or teaching. For the Jewish Christian audience of this book, the controversy was not between being Jewish and being Christian. The controversy was *within* Jewish tradition about a new development in that tradition.

Literary Context

Particularly important in Hebrews are the author's use of Scripture, the role of comparisons in the author's argument, Hebrews' Jewish and Greek contexts, the author's conviction that Jesus Christ is Lord, and the author's determination to impress the importance of this conviction upon the original audience members, who are flagging in their faith.

Throughout Hebrews, the author compares God's revelation in Jesus Christ with what has gone before. The comparison is particularly with God's word spoken through prophets in Hebrew scriptures (notably Moses) and with temple practices and ritual traditions.

The **Hellenistic** context is also important. Hebrews draws on contemporary Greek thought in which what is diverse is inferior to what is singular, temporary is inferior to eternal, mortal is inferior to immortal, created is inferior to creator, human is inferior to divine, and changing is inferior to unchanging or final.

This **dualistic** world of ideas is reflected in how the writer tells about Jesus. Using these ideas and Hebrew scripture, the author argues that God's speaking in Jesus is superior to what has gone before. Jesus is superior to **angels,** Moses, and priests; the new covenant is superior to the old; and Jesus as sacrifice is superior to previous sacrifices. The author uses contemporary ideas to express realities beyond the ideas. For example, in chapters 1 and 2 the author uses both Hellenistic and Hebrew traditions and ideas to argue that Jesus is both fully divine and fully human, an idea that was foreign to both contemporary Hellenistic and Hebrew thought and traditions.

Lutheran Context

Martin Luther had mixed feelings about the letter to the Hebrews (which we will discuss further in a later session). As a Hebrew Bible scholar, Luther admired the book, describing it as "a marvelously fine epistle. It discusses Christ's priesthood masterfully and profoundly on the basis of the Scriptures and extensively interprets the Old Testament in a fine way. . . . It is the work of an able and learned man; . . . greatly experienced in faith and practiced in the Scriptures." The author "discloses a firm grasp of the reading of the Scriptures and of the proper way of dealing with them" (preface to the Epistle to the Hebrews 1546 [1522] in "Word and Sacrament," *Luther's Works* 35:394-95).

Hellenistic:
Hellenistic refers to the Greek culture that had wide influence beginning in the late fourth century B.C.E. in the Mediterranean region, including areas of what we refer to as the Near East and northern Africa. The term derives from the Greek word *Hellen*, which is the Greeks' name for themselves.

Dualistic:
Dualistic is a characteristic of some philosophical and theological traditions that divides reality into opposites (good and evil, human and divine, earthly and heavenly, male and female, right and wrong).

Angel:
In both Greek and Hebrew, the words we translate as *angel* simply mean "messenger."

SESSION ONE

The "proper way of dealing" with Scripture has changed over time. Through the centuries, people have developed many methods of biblical interpretation. Hebrews frequently quotes from or alludes to the Hebrew scriptures to make an argument. The author's use of Scripture reflects a method of interpretation well respected in its time and suspect in our own. For readers today, the *scriptural context* of a text is crucial for understanding its meaning. The method of interpretation found in Hebrews regarded each word, as well as each verse, chapter, and book, as having important meaning *apart from its scriptural context* or setting.

For Lutherans, as for most Christians, Jesus Christ is the lens through whom we read. The life, death, and resurrection of Jesus Christ give us the basis for understanding Scripture.

Devotional Context

The author of Hebrews describes Christ's divinity in a number of ways. Christ is first of all Son of God and, hence, superior to the angels. To be a "son" is to have the attributes of the parent or original person, to share in that person's being.

Christ is heir of that which God created as well as sustains. God created the worlds through the Son from the beginning. God appointed the Son heir of all things into the future. As the reflection of God's glory and the exact imprint of God's very being, Christ is like Hebrew tradition's **Wisdom**. Wisdom is described as "a reflection of eternal light, a spotless mirror of the working of God, and an image of his [sic] goodness. Although she [sic] is but one, she can do all things, and while remaining in herself, she renews all things" (Wisdom of Solomon 7:26-27a). Christ sustains all things by his powerful word, which is God's own Word. In this, Christ is the contemporary Greek thought's *Logos* by which God sustains the world. The author uses both Wisdom from Hebrew tradition and the *Logos*—or "Word"—from Greek tradition to point to Jesus as God. "Glory" is another specific reference to the divine reality in which Christ participates.

> **? Wisdom:**
> In Hebrew tradition, Wisdom is a female personification of God's being. Scriptural traditions assign Wisdom's attributes to Jesus. Jesus spoke of himself in these terms. Wisdom in Hebrew tradition and the *Logos* in Greek tradition have similarities, which the author of Hebrews uses to describe Jesus as God.

SESSION ONE

Facilitator's Prayer

According to your great love, you created me and everyone who will gather for this time together. You have given us your Word in Scripture and in Jesus. You speak to us in Word and in Jesus. Jesus is your voice, your breath, yourself. As we study your word, give us that breath to breathe, help us to hear your voice. Teach us to speak you and your love to one another. Amen.

Gather (10-15 minutes)

Check-in

Take time to greet each person and invite learners to introduce themselves to one another.

 Tip: Taking a few moments for check-in is well worth it. Without an opportunity to settle in, even unload a bit from the day, learners may be distracted and less able to focus. Sharing the day's challenges lightens the burden. Sharing the day's celebrations likewise brings people together.

Pray

God of heaven and earth, before the foundation of the universe and the beginning of time you are the triune God: Author of creation, eternal Word of salvation, life-giving Spirit of wisdom. Guide us to all truth by your Spirit, that we may proclaim all that Christ has revealed and rejoice in the glory he shares with us. Glory and praise to you, Father, Son, and Holy Spirit, now and forever. Amen. (*Evangelical Lutheran Worship*, second option for prayer of the day for Trinity Sunday, p. 37)

Focus Activity

Quickly write down three words that describe God. Then take a few minutes to meditate on these words as descriptions of Jesus.

 Tip: Be mindful that participants will vary in their understanding of Jesus' divinity. For some it will be unquestionable. Others may not really have thought about it much. For some it will be a challenge to think of Jesus as God. What's most important is to listen and hear one another's approaches to this central theological issue.

Open Scripture (10-15 minutes)

For this reading, have two readers—one to read the "narrator" parts and one to read the scripture quotations.

Ask someone to read the passage at a normal pace. Then have learners close their eyes to listen while another person reads the passage very slowly.

SESSION ONE

> Read Hebrews 1:1-14.
> - What words stand out most to you?
> - What questions do you have?
> - What is your emotional reaction?

Join the Conversation (25-55 minutes)

Historical Context

1. Hebrews, one of the latest books of the Bible, was written sometime between 60 and 100 C.E., approximately 30 to 70 years after Jesus' death. This means some in the original audience were probably second- or even third-generation followers of Jesus Christ.

Imagine yourself in the original audience, raised in the Christian faith from childhood, and now perhaps taking your faith for granted or neglecting it. You may be facing a hostile environment and growing weary of being faithful.

- Make a list of things that might be distracting you, not only from the faith, but also from other important aspects of your life, such as time with family and friends, sleep, and your favorite renewing activities.
- Brainstorm a list of things you could do in this situation to help bring your life back into focus.

2. The conversation of which Hebrews is a part is a conversation *within* a community of Jewish Christians. The controversy is not between being Jewish and being Christian. It is *within* Jewish tradition about a new development in that tradition. And so, throughout Hebrews, the author compares God's revelation in Jesus Christ with what has gone before in God's Word spoken through prophets in Hebrew scriptures, temple practices, and ritual traditions. In Hebrews 1:5-14, for example, a series of psalms (Psalm 2:7; 104:4; 45:6-7; 102:25-27; and 110:1) refer to Christ.

- How do you suppose the original audience reacted to this use of Hebrew scriptures?
- How does this connection between Hebrew scriptures and Christ affect your reading of Hebrews 1:1-14?

Tip:
Be mindful that some learners may be wavering in their faith just as the original audience of Hebrews was. Sharing in this Bible study may even be their first step toward strengthening and reaffirming their faith.

Bonus Activity:
Just as the author of Hebrews used Greek philosophical thought as part of his discussion of Jesus, in other times and places contemporary modes of thinking contribute to understanding of faith. As an example, ask participants to share ways in which contemporary science contributes to their understanding of God and to their faith.

Bonus Activity:
Have participants take a few moments of quiet meditation to recall and give thanks for the people who introduced them to Christian faith and for those who helped sustain their faith in challenging times. You may want to have some participants share their reflections.

Literary Context

1. Throughout the book of Hebrews, you will find the author making comparisons. Signals for the comparisons are words such as *new, superior, better, more, excellent,* and the conjunction *but*.

- Review Hebrews 1:1-14. Find and list the comparisons in the text. What points do these comparisons make?

2. One of the concerns of Hebrews is to describe fully the person of Jesus. The author worships Jesus as Lord, and wants the audience to share that conviction.

- List the words in Hebrews 1:1-14 that describe Jesus. How do these descriptions assert that Jesus is Lord?

Lutheran Context

1. One Lutheran principle for reading and interpreting the Bible is the question, "What shows forth Christ?" Martin Luther says the Bible is like the manger holding the Christ child. Everything in the Bible points us and leads us to Christ.

- What do you think about the idea that everything in the Bible draws us to Christ?
- How does Hebrews 1:1-14 point you or lead you to Christ?

2. Another Lutheran principle for reading and interpreting the Bible is "Scripture interprets Scripture." To gain a better understanding of challenging passages of Scripture, we can look at related texts.

- Read John 1:1-3; 1 Corinthians 8:6; and Colossians 1:15-20. How do these texts affect your understanding of Hebrews 1:1-14? List what each text says about the relationship between God and Jesus.

Bonus Activity:

Read the scriptures quoted in Hebrews and their contexts. Discuss how this affects your understanding of the scripture quotations and of Hebrews 1:1-14.

Verses in Hebrews 1	Quoted from	Contexts
5	Psalm 2:7 and 2 Samuel 7:14	Psalm 2; 2 Samuel 7:1-17
6	Deuteronomy 32:43	Deuteronomy 32:36-43
7	Psalm 104:4	Psalm 104:1-9
8-9	Psalm 45:6-7	Psalm 45:1-10
10-12	Psalm 102:25-27	Psalm 102
13	Psalm 110:1	Psalm 110:1-7

Tip:

In this session text and throughout the series, encourage participants to note Hebrews' use of comparisons, which are signaled by such words as *new, superior, better, more,* and *excellent*.

Bonus Activity:

Use the list of descriptions of Jesus compiled in the discussion. Ask participants what place, if any, each of these words or phrases has in their personal understanding of Jesus and their faith. What other terms would they use to describe Jesus as Lord? What contemporary words and images—unknown at the time of Hebrews—can help translate what Hebrews is saying?

Tip:

People vary in their approaches to Scripture. Don't think that you need to resolve these differences. Help participants to listen to one another's differing perspectives. Help people to look for Jesus in the text and in their exchanges with one another.

SESSION ONE

 Bonus Activity:

Luther referred to "a canon within the canon." That is, certain portions of Scripture or whole books are more central than others. They become part of our interpretive lens for all of Scripture. For Luther, John's Gospel, John 1, Paul's letters, and 1 Peter "are the books that show you Christ and teach you all that is necessary for you to know, even if you were never to see or hear any other book of doctrine" (preface to the New Testament 1546 [1522], in "Word and Sacrament," *Luther's Works* 35:362). Ask participants whether particular verses or books are central to their faith. If so, ask them to share what these are and how they are important.

 Bonus Activity:

The author of Hebrews quotes Scripture a lot to make his argument. Ask participants to share stories of Bible verses that were shared with them in their lives to make a point—and whether this worked!

 Bonus Activity:

Read aloud the Nicene Creed's second article—the section particularly about Jesus (*ELW*, p. 104; *LBW*, p. 84). Ask participants to compare this statement of faith with chapter 1 of Hebrews. Identify the similarities and differences. What questions does this raise?

 Tip:

People vary in their devotional lives and relationship to Jesus Christ, whom some may relate to more as divine and others more as human. Or, for a particular person, this may vary over time and circumstances. Listen generously, aware that in the next session Jesus' humanity will be the focus.

Devotional Context

1. Take a moment to get quiet and comfortable. Look at the Focus Image for this session. Close your eyes for a few moments and hold the image in your mind's eye. Then share with another person what you see in the painting. What do you notice first? What emotional response do you have to the painting?

2. Sing together the first verse of "All Hail the Power of Jesus' Name!" (*LBW* 328, 329; *ELW* 634). Then sing together "You Are Holy" (*ELW* 525). How do these songs tell you that Jesus is Lord of all?

Wrap-up

1. Recall the list of titles and descriptions for Jesus. Note other descriptors that have been mentioned in the course of the discussion.

2. Ask participants to share questions that they have coming out of this session. Make note of them in case they can be addressed as the study moves along.

Pray

Power of the eternal Father, help me. Wisdom of the Son, enlighten the eye of my understanding. Tender mercy of the Holy Spirit, unite my heart to yourself. Eternal God, restore health to the sick and life to the dead. Give us a voice, your own voice, to cry out to you for mercy for the world. You, light, give us light. You, wisdom, give us wisdom. You, supreme strength, strengthen us. Amen. ("A prayer of Catherine of Siena," *Evangelical Lutheran Worship*, p. 87)

SESSION ONE

Extending the Conversation (5 minutes)

Homework

1. Read the next session's Bible text: Hebrews 2:5-18.

2. Use what you learned and experienced in this session in daily devotions this week. In daily prayer, give thanks for knowing God in Jesus. Sing or recite aloud one of the hymns included in the session. Repeating the song "You Are Holy" several times can be a meditation in itself. Each day write a one-sentence prayer to God about yourself and your faith.

3. We are surrounded by distractions from what is most important to us. A minor crisis or sense of urgency about secondary commitments can distract us from our primary commitments. An advertisement can pull us toward things, activities, or people who aren't really important to us. Ruffled feelings can distract us from focusing on what's at the heart of an interaction. Weariness or a short temper can distract us from kindness and understanding. At the start of the week, make a list of the three or four people, relationships, activities, attitudes, or needs that are the highest priorities for your life, especially for your life this week. As you go about your daily activities this week, note how you are distracted. Being aware of distractions is part of learning to affirm and focus on what's most important.

Enrichment

1. If you want to read through the entire book of Hebrews during this unit, read the following sections this week.
Day 1: Hebrews 1:1-4
Day 2: Hebrews 1:5-14
Day 3: Hebrews 2:1-4
Day 4: Hebrews 2:5-9
Day 5: Hebrews 2:10-13
Day 6: Hebrews 2:14-18
Day 7: Hebrews 3:1-6

2. Many artists—painters, sculptors, composers, and others—have tried to convey Jesus' divinity. Search out and explore some of these on the Web or at your local library.

3. The Bible tells us that humanity is created in God's image (Genesis 1:26). Make a list of the descriptions of Jesus' divinity or highlight the descriptions in your Bible. They tell us something about God, in whose image we are created. What do these descriptions tell us about who we are? What do these descriptions tell us about others?

Tip:
Hebrews is a text that will raise substantial questions, not all of which will be answered or even addressed in this series. Emphasize that the life of faith is an ongoing conversation with Scripture. Encourage participants to read the entire book pf Jebreusing the suggested schedule of readings. Encourage them also to follow up with further reading and other activities.

SESSION ONE

> **For Further Reading**
>
> *A History of God: The 4,000-Year Quest of Judaism, Christianity and Islam* by Karen Armstrong (New York: Ballantine, 1994).
>
> Available at augsburgfortress.org:
>
> *Hebrews for Everyone* by N. T. Wright (Minneapolis: Augsburg Fortress, 2004).

Looking Ahead

1. Read the next session's Bible text: Hebrews 2:5-18.

2. Read through the Leader Guide for the next session and mark portions you wish to highlight for the group.

3. Make a checklist of any materials you'll need to do the Bonus Activities.

4. Pray for members of your group during the week.

5. As you prepare, be aware of the questions and concerns that arise for you, which will give you a heads-up about you may expect from others in the next session.

SESSION TWO

Hebrews 2:5-18

Leader Session Guide

Focus Statement

The person Jesus Christ is fully human, in every way like us. In Jesus we see and know God. In Jesus we see and know who God created us to be.

Key Verse

Therefore he had to become like his brothers and sisters in every respect, so that he might be a merciful and faithful high priest in the service of God, to make a sacrifice of atonement for the sins of the people.
Hebrews 2:17

Focus Image

© Design Pics/SuperStock

Who Is Jesus? (Part 2)

Session Preparation

Before You Begin . . .

Take a few moments to consider what it means to be human. Reflect on phrases like "I'm only human," "she's a real human being," "the milk of human kindness," "human frailty," and "it's human nature." Consider what's important to you personally about being human. What are your feelings as you reflect on this?

Session Instructions

1. Read this Session Guide completely and highlight or underline any portions you wish to emphasize with the group. Note any Bonus Activities you wish to do.

2. If you plan to do any special activities, check to see what materials you'll need, if any.

3. Have extra Bibles on hand in case a member of the group forgets to bring one.

Session Overview

Jesus' humanity is as important to the author of Hebrews as Jesus' divinity. This session explores both what Hebrews has to say about Jesus' humanity and the church's understanding of Jesus being both human and divine. Martin Luther put a great emphasis on Jesus' humanity, teaching that it is through Jesus' humanity and our own that we truly know God.

HISTORICAL CONTEXT

The **incarnation**—Christianity's teaching that Jesus is both human and divine—burst the confines of both Greek philosophical thought and Hebrew tradition. Ancient Greek philosophy knows God as immutable and, therefore, impersonal. The Hebrew scriptural tradition teaches that God interacts with human beings in history. God walked in the garden with Adam and Eve. God spoke to Moses in the wilderness.

This seemingly irreconcilable difference came to a head in the fourth century in the Arian controversy. Arius was an elder of the church at Alexandria. Arius and his followers taught that God is impersonal and outside history, while God's *Logos* is personal and directly involved with human beings. The *Logos* ("word"

SESSION TWO

> **? Incarnation:**
> "Incarnation" is embodiment in flesh (Latin: *caro, carnis*). In Christianity, the incarnation is the belief that God was flesh and blood in Jesus.

in Greek) refers to Jesus. For example, John 1:1 says of Jesus, "In the beginning was the Word, and the Word was with God, and the Word was God." This last idea—that the Word Jesus is God—was the focus of the Arian controversy. Did the *Logos* of God exist coeternally with God the Father, or was there a time when the *Logos* did not exist? Is the *Logos* a creation of God and less divine? Or, is the *Logos* uncreated and fully divine? What is God's relationship to the world? Are creator and creation separate, or is the creator intimately involved in the creation?

The Roman emperor Constantine called the First Ecumenical Council in 325 C.E. to resolve the controversy, which was dividing the Roman Empire. The First and Second (381 C.E.) Ecumenical Councils gave the church the Nicene Creed, which articulated a resolution to the dispute.

LITERARY CONTEXT

Note the ways in which the author points to Jesus' humanity. Having earlier argued that Jesus is superior to angels, we hear now that "for a little while" Jesus was made "lower than the angels," that is, human. As a human being, Jesus' suffering and death are the focus of the author's attention. Jesus shared "flesh and blood," which meant he was subject to death like all human beings. "Like his brothers and sisters in every respect," Jesus "was tested by what he suffered." Seeing Jesus—that Jesus is visible, not invisible—is also a mark of his humanity.

> **? Sanctified:**
> To be "sanctified" is to be made holy. To be holy is to belong to God. In our sanctification, Jesus, Son of God, accomplished our adoption as children of God.

Note that Jesus is described as "pioneer" of salvation. In ancient Greece, a pioneer or leader was the founder of a city, fellowship, or community. As pioneer, Jesus' work of "perfecting" and **"sanctifying"** as "merciful and faithful high priest in the service of God" making "sacrifice of atonement" will be discussed more fully later in Hebrews and in the next session of this study. The motifs of high priest and sacrifice are based in Hebrew liturgical and scriptural tradition.

In Hebrews 2:9, Jesus' humanity and his being "crowned with glory and honor" are tied together. Likewise, in verse 10, Jesus' "bringing many children to glory" is connected with his suffering.

The motifs of freedom and slavery were central in Hebrew tradition. The God who raised Jesus from the dead—freeing human beings from the death and the power of death—was the God who delivered—and delivers—slaves from bondage.

SESSION TWO

LUTHERAN CONTEXT

We know God most clearly in the person of Jesus. In his lectures on Hebrews, Luther said, "Therefore he who wants to ascend advantageously to the love and knowledge of God should abandon the human metaphysical rules concerning knowledge of the divinity and apply himself first to the humanity of Christ. For it is exceedingly godless temerity that, where God has humiliated Himself in order to become recognizable, man seeks for himself another way by following the counsels of his own natural capacity" (Lectures on Hebrews, *Luther's Works* 29:111).

Luther goes further, saying that it is not just Jesus himself who is God's revelation to us. Because God was flesh and blood among us in Jesus Christ, we can know God in flesh and blood, that is, in other people and in ourselves.

Jesus being fully human and fully divine is a **paradox**. The identification of Jesus' humiliation with Jesus' exaltation is a paradox. Not only Jesus' becoming human but also Jesus' suffering and death on the cross are the grounds of Jesus' exaltation. "[God] exalted Christ above all things when He cast Him down below all things" (Lectures on Hebrews, *Luther's Works* 29:127).

Jesus' humanity, God's being in flesh and blood, fulfills God's plan of salvation. In suffering and dying, Jesus became like all human beings so that human beings could become like Jesus in glory and honor.

DEVOTIONAL CONTEXT

Death and fear are powerful realities in our lives. Yet, Jesus became incarnate "so that through death he might destroy the one who has the power of death, that is, the devil, and free those who all their lives were held in slavery by the fear of death" (Hebrews 2:14-15). In Jesus Christ we need no longer fear death. "The devil," the power of evil, has been overcome.

Participants may or may not believe there is or ever was such a being as the "devil." Either way, they may question the devil's having been overcome, given the state of the world. Hebrews' approach to the problem of evil being overcome is "already, not yet." In Hebrews 2:8, the author writes, "Now in subjecting all things to [human beings], God left nothing outside their control." Of course, none of us feels everything is under control, much less that we have control over everything. Hebrews goes on, "As it is,

 Paradox:
A paradox is a statement that contradicts itself.

SESSION TWO

we do not yet see everything in subjection to them, but we do see Jesus." Jesus' suffering, death, and resurrection—his humiliation and exaltation—are evidence to us that, despite appearances, death is not the final word.

Facilitator's Prayer

Gracious and loving God, give me grace and generosity as I lead Bible study. Help me to see you in every person who gathers for this time together. And, let me, by my words and actions, be a witness to your love for us all. Amen.

Gather (10-15 minutes)

Check-in

Tip:
Listen carefully for any comments people have regarding the previous week's session or their follow-up experiences during the week. You may be able to draw on these in this or later sessions.

Invite learners to share completed homework or any new thoughts or insights about the previous session. Be ready to give a brief recap of that session if necessary.

Pray

Almighty God, you gave us your only Son to take on our human nature and to illumine the world with your light. By your grace adopt us as your children and enlighten us with your Spirit, through Jesus Christ, our Redeemer and Lord, who lives and reigns with you and the Holy Spirit, one God, now and forever. Amen. (Nativity of Our Lord III, *ELW*, p. 20)

Focus Activity

Tip:
Be mindful that participants come with different physical abilities. If it will be helpful, accommodate participants by their location in the room or type of seating.

Take a moment to focus on Jesus as fully human. Stand or sit. Close your eyes. Focus on your posture—the angle of your head, the positions of your arms and legs, the shape of your back. Imagine that you are Jesus. Adjust your body as you imagine what it felt like to be him. What does it feel like? How is this different from your usual stance or posture?

Open Scripture (10-15 minutes)

Form two or three groups. Have members of each group work together to present the text in a creative way for the rest of the participants. After the creative presentation, explore the similarities and differences among the groups' approaches.

Use sketch books to have listeners "doodle" during the reading. It's useful for visible learners to "see" what they are hearing.

Read Hebrews 2:5-18.
- How do you feel as you hear this passage?
- What word or phrase in the text grabs your attention most?
- What questions does the text raise for you?

Join the Conversation (25-55 minutes)

Historical Context

1. Hebrews expresses the belief that God was flesh and blood in Jesus. This belief, called the *incarnation*, burst the confines of both Greek philosophical thought and Hebrew tradition.
- Read together the Nicene Creed. Look closely at the Second Article, the portion about Jesus. How does it talk about Jesus' humanity? What is the relationship between Jesus' humanity and Jesus' divinity in this creed?
- Look also at the Apostles' Creed, a shorter creed from an earlier time in the church. List differences and similarities in how this creed and the Nicene Creed teach the relationship between Jesus' divinity and humanity.

Literary Context

1. While Hebrews 1 emphasizes Jesus as divine, Hebrews 2 emphasizes Jesus as human.
- Read Hebrews 2:5-18 and underline or highlight the words and phrases that distinguish Jesus as human.

2. Jesus is described as the "pioneer" of salvation (Hebrews 2:10) and later as the "pioneer" of our faith (Hebrews 12:2). Pioneers may lead the way or break new ground in fields such as science, technology, music, or dance. Some pioneers are explorers—on earth or in space. Some pioneers are the "first," for example, the first female major league baseball umpire.

 Bonus Activity:
Distribute copies of the Athanasian Creed (*LBW*, pp. 54-55). Have the group read it aloud, each participant in turn reading a sentence. Ask for initial responses to the creed. Ask participants to speculate about the theological controversy or controversies that may have given rise to this creed. As there is time, have participants underline the word *Son* wherever it occurs, and then focus on what the creed has to say about the Son.

 Tip:
Mention that controversies have marked the church throughout its entire history. They are part of the process of discernment in our life together. What seems settled—even obvious—to us now may once have been the object of great conflict.

 Bonus Activity:
Philippians 2:5-11 is an ancient creedal hymn about Jesus' human and divine nature. Ask participants to close their eyes and visualize the text as a volunteer reads it aloud slowly two times. After a few moments, ask participants what they experienced, saw, or learned in this visualization.

 Tip:
Encourage participants to underline or highlight words or phrases and to make notes in the margins of their Bibles. Some people will be a bit uncomfortable with the idea. The Word of God is not confined to the page, which is only a vehicle for our receiving it. The Bible—God's Word—is an invitation to conversation and engagement, including on the page itself.

SESSION TWO

Bonus Activity:
Jesus was in every way like us. Have participants read Matthew 26:39 and Matthew 27:46, then discuss whether Jesus experienced fear. By what he did (which will be discussed further in the next session), Jesus freed "those who all their lives were held in slavery by the fear of death" (Hebrews 2:15).

Bonus Activity:
Jesus "shared the same things"—our flesh and blood—and became "like his brothers and sisters in every respect" (Hebrews 2:14-17). Explore these images. Invite participants to close their eyes and get a clear image in their minds of a particularly memorable experience. Then, in their minds, invite them to put Jesus in their place, experiencing what they experienced.

Tip:
Some Christians find it difficult to accept the idea that God died. For others, God's dying only makes clearer God's power over death and God's willingness to become vulnerable for our sake.

Bonus Activity:
Invite participants to express their views on whether God died on the cross. Record responses—yes "votes," no "votes," and other comments. A few early theologians taught that God the Father and God the Son were the same, so the Father suffered and died just as the Son did. Ecumenical councils distinguished the Father and the Son. The Son suffered and died; the Father did not. In more recent centuries, theologians (including Luther) have articulated the idea that though the Father did not die, God did die since the Son is God. What does it mean that God died? For Luther, God's suffering was a mystery, which he understood as a paradox.

- Draw or describe what the word *pioneer* means to you. What does a pioneer do? Where does a pioneer go? What are followers' relationships to a pioneer? What kind of person does it take to be a pioneer?
- What does the image of a pioneer tell us about Jesus?

Lutheran Context

1. Lutheran theology includes several *paradoxes*—statements or realities that seem to contradict themselves. (For example, Martin Luther talked about Scripture as both law and gospel, and Christians as both saints and sinners.) The session Scripture text also contains paradoxes: Jesus is fully human and fully divine, and he is exalted because he becomes human and suffers and dies on the cross. As Luther writes, "[God] exalted Christ above all things when He cast Him down below all things" (Lectures on Hebrews, *Luther's Works* 29:127).

- How does the paradox of Jesus' full humanity and divinity help you and your faith?
- List the questions this paradox raises for you.

2. For Luther, becoming a parent brought with it faith lessons. In his children, Luther realized what it meant that God was born among us in Jesus Christ, an infant child.

- Identify ways in which human infants are vulnerable and dependent.
- How does it feel to imagine God as a human infant?

Devotional Context

1. Sing together "Word of God, Come Down on Earth" (*ELW* 510). Then, as someone reads the words aloud slowly and deliberately, stand when the hymn refers to Jesus' humanity and sit when it refers to Jesus' divinity.

2. Sometimes people think of Jesus as somehow superhuman. Rather, Jesus is *fully* human. In Jesus, we see what God intends for human beings. Jesus is fully human and, in our human sinfulness, we fall short of being fully human. Write in a journal or make a picture of ways in which you feel or sense this in your life, and ways in which Jesus shows what it means to be fully human.

3. Turn your attention to the session's Focus Image. Imagine yourself as part of the scene. Describe what you experience and the emotions this evokes.

Wrap-up

1. If there are any questions to explore further, write them on chart paper or a whiteboard. Ask for volunteers to do further research to share with the group at the next session.

2. Ask each person who is willing to briefly tell one embarrassing thing about themselves. After each person is done sharing, have the group say together, "Jesus was human, just like you."

3. Review the ways Jesus' humanity has been described in this session. Ask participants if they want to add anything to this.

Pray

Brother Jesus, you are like me. Does that mean I am like you? In the week ahead, help me to follow your lead. And, in the week ahead, strengthen me in the face of challenges, that I may meet them with love and without fear, because I am confident in your love. Amen.

Extending the Conversation (5 minutes)

Homework

1. Read the next session's Bible text: Hebrews 4:14—5:10; 9:24—10:1; 10:10-18.

2. Created in God's image, you have a body! This week celebrate your body—the fact that you are incarnate! Exercise as you are able—flex your feet and ankles right now, go for a walk this week, stretch your arms and legs as you are sitting. Make physical contact with people who are important to you and, as you do, thank God you are human. Eat responsibly. Take deep breaths. As you perform life's daily bodily care and preparations, celebrate these basic human realities as part of who God made you to be.

3. As you hear news of human suffering, pray for the people involved and their care and healing. Pray for peace. If you are able, do something to help alleviate suffering. Perhaps you can make a contribution of money. Perhaps you will write a letter to encourage legislative action. You may very well meet human suffering face-to-face in this week and have an opportunity to be of help more directly. When you see suffering, remember that Jesus is there.

Bonus Activity:
In 1996, the song "One of Us" was in the top 10 on the pop music charts. This song was written by Eric Bazilian and originally recorded by Joan Osborne and later by Alanis Morissette. The questioning refrain, "What if God was one of us?" can help you and your group reflect on the incarnation. Obtain a recording of the song and play it for your group. Note the questions in the song and discuss them.

Tip:
For the reflection on the Focus Image, quiet the room and encourage everyone to get comfortable. Invite participants to meditate on the Focus Image as a volunteer slowly reads aloud the following passages: Hebrews 2:9; 1 John 4:18; Romans 8:15; and Hebrews 2:18. As a closing to your meditation, pass the peace among the group.

Tip:
Use this opportunity to bring together the themes of the first two sessions, which have focused on the person of Jesus Christ, who is fully divine and fully human.

Tip:
The question for the next session is "What did Jesus do?" Suggest that participants note how that question is answered in the Bible texts for the session.

SESSION TWO

Enrichment

1. If you want to read through the entire book of Hebrews during this unit, read the following sections this week.
Day 1: Hebrews 3:7-19
Day 2: Hebrews 4:1-11
Day 3: Hebrews 4:12-13
Day 4: Hebrews 4:14-16
Day 5: Hebrews 5:1-6
Day 6: Hebrews 5:7-14
Day 7: Hebrews 6:1-12

2. Do a Web search to learn more about the Arian controversy. For example, the First Ecumenical Council was called by the Roman emperor Constantine. What business did an emperor have convening a Christian assembly?

3. *The Green Mile* (Castle Rock Entertainment, 1999) is a film based on a Stephen King serial novel (Signet, 1996) of the same title. The story takes place on death row. The characters are guards and inmates, one of whom has special powers. That character, John Coffey, convicted of a heinous crime of which he is innocent, is both intimidating and childlike. *The Green Mile* is a story of how people respond in the face of human and divine powers at work in their midst, a story of great cruelty and great healing. Watch the film with others or, if you participate in a book group, suggest reading the novel.

For Further Reading

And the Word Became History by Medardo Ernesto Gómez (Minneapolis: Augsburg, 1992).

The Gospel According to Jesus Christ by José Saramago (San Diego: Harvest Books, 1994).

Looking Ahead

1. Read the next session's Bible text: 4:14—5:10; 9:24—10:1; 10:10-18.

2. Read through the Leader Guide for the next session and mark portions you wish to highlight for the group.

3. Make a checklist of any materials you'll need to do the Bonus Activities

4. Pray for members of your group during the week.

SESSION THREE

Hebrews 4:14—
5:10; 9:24—10:1;
10:10-18

Leader Session Guide

 Focus Statement

Because of who Jesus is—human and divine—Jesus is priest in both earth and heaven, in history and for eternity. By his obedience to God's work, Jesus perfected faith and fulfilled God's plan for our salvation.

 Key Verse

Since, then, we have a great high priest who has passed through the heavens, Jesus, the Son of God, let us hold fast to our confession. For we do not have a high priest who is unable to sympathize with our weaknesses, but we have one who in every respect has been tested as we are, yet without sin. Hebrews 4:14-15

 Focus Image

© BilderLounge / SuperStock

What Did Jesus Do?

Session Preparation

Before You Begin . . .

As you prepare for this session, reflect for a moment on your strengths and weaknesses. Make a list in your mind or on paper. Say aloud to yourself which strength you most enjoy. Say aloud to yourself which weakness most bothers you. Pray thanks for your strengths and your weaknesses. In your mind's eye, put your strengths and weaknesses in a basket and hand them to Jesus.

Session Instructions

1. Read this Session Guide completely and highlight or underline any portions you wish to emphasize with the group. Note any Bonus Activities you wish to do.

2. If you plan to do any special activities, check to see what materials you'll need, if any.

3. Have extra Bibles on hand in case a member of the group forgets to bring one.

Session Overview

Having focused on who Jesus is, we turn now to what Jesus did. Hebrews compares Jesus with the high priest Melchizedek, Jesus' priesthood with the levitical priesthood, and Jesus' **sacrifice** with traditional sacrifice. In all the comparisons, the author's intent is to show that Jesus accomplished once and for all what no one else could accomplish. Through who he was and what he did, Jesus accomplished our salvation.

HISTORICAL CONTEXT

In one Hebrew tradition, priests came from among the descendants of Levi and were called Levites or levitical priests. In another tradition, the priests were descendants of Moses' brother Aaron. Traditions vary about whether Aaron was a Levite, but he was the first high priest. Provisions in Leviticus appointing Aaron give a formal description of the role of high priest. Hebrews' discussion of Jesus as high priest relates to the Leviticus description.

The primary role of priests was to serve God. Priests were intermediaries who spoke to God on behalf of the people and to the people on behalf of God. Some, notably the high priest, served God at the community's primary site of worship, the

SESSION THREE

> **? Sacrifice:**
> A sacrifice is a slaughtered animal offered to a deity. The offering is itself also called a sacrifice. The sacrifice might be understood to appease the deity's wrath, to atone for sin, or to pay a penalty for misdoing. Both Hebrew scripture and tradition prescribe sacrifice and tell of God's rejection of the practice. Elements of the process of sacrifice are present in Holy Communion or the Eucharist: the offering, the slaughtered victim, the victim's blood, the meal, and the atonement or reconciliation.

> **? Obedience:**
> In English as well as Hebrew and Greek, obedience has to do with hearing. Obedience is hearing and responding or hearing with one's whole self, the way you turn your attention when someone calls your name across a room. What one hears becomes integrated into one's life. Disobedience, on the other hand, is not responding to what one hears.

> **? Perfect:**
> Hebrews does not use "perfect" in a moral sense. Perfect here means complete, fulfilled, or mature. For example: "He is a perfect fool." "She's perfect for the job." "It's perfect for the task." Jesus' perfection is in having fulfilled God's Word. Jesus perfects our salvation by fully accomplishing it according to God's plan. Jesus perfects our faith by making it complete and whole. When believers are exhorted to "go on toward perfection" (Hebrews 6:1), they are encouraged to mature in faith.

Jerusalem temple while it was standing. The high priest played a particularly important role in the community's annual rite of sacrifice and renewal, when the priest made sacrifices to atone for his own sins and the sins of all the people. Leviticus 16–17 describes this Day of Atonement or, in Hebrew, Yom Kippur.

Participants may be familiar with the high priest or chief priest of Gospel stories. For example, in Matthew 26, Jesus is tried before the high priest Caiaphas. In the Gospels, the high priests were enemies of Jesus and were part of the plot on his life. Distinguish the high priest of the Gospels from the high priest of Leviticus 16–17.

Literary Context

Hebrews 4:14—5:10 lays out a comparison that will be elaborated on in other portions of this session. We're reminded that Jesus is both divine (passing through the heavens, Son of God, sinless) and human (tested, able to sympathize with weakness, flesh, suffering). The high priests, beginning with Aaron, were chosen from among mortals. The high priests are like Jesus in their humanity and unlike Jesus in his divinity.

Jesus is likened to Melchizedek. Important to this comparison are that Melchizedek's priesthood lasts forever (Psalm 110:4) and he appears out of nowhere to bless and rename Abram and then disappears (Genesis 14:17-20).

Jesus' **obedience** is as important as Jesus' having been made **perfect**. Jesus hears God's Word with his entire being, and he completely fulfills God's purpose.

Hebrews 9:24—10:1 emphasizes the perfection of Jesus' service as high priest. Jesus' service was not repeated but was done once and for all—his offering, his suffering, his sacrifice. That Jesus' earthly service was also heavenly service is witnessed in the contrast of "human hands," "mere copy," and "shadow" with "true," "heaven," and "the presence of God." While other priests performed their service in historically limited, earthly reality, Jesus' service was cosmic.

Hebrews 10:10-18 continues the affirmation of Jesus' work as high priest and identifies Jesus' sacrifice with his exaltation. Crucial in Jesus' work is that "by a single offering he has perfected for all time those who are sanctified" (Hebrews 10:14). Jesus' work was to make us whole.

SESSION THREE

Lutheran Context

In Hebrews' terms, Jesus as high priest made atonement for all our sins once and for all. For Luther, this is the heart of the gospel, that our sins are forgiven. From the cross, Jesus said, "It is finished" (John 19:30). Jesus accomplished this work on the cross, where he offered himself for our sake, and was exalted.

The personal dimension of Jesus' work is crucial. Luther emphasized the importance of believing not only that Jesus did this work for us but also that Jesus did this work *for you*. Salvation is *for you*.

Jesus' work also has implications for pastoral ministry. The pastor (or, priest, as Luther had it) ministers not on behalf of himself or herself but on behalf of others. Anointing—for us, ordination—is "not so much for the purpose of being worthy to touch the sacrament of the body of Christ as [for the purpose of dealing] gently with the matter of the same sacrament, that is, with the people of Christ" (Lectures on Hebrews, *Luther's Works* 29:170).

The implications of Jesus' work for our worship are important: "Absolutely nothing external is of value to the soul" (Lectures on Hebrews, *Luther's Works* 29:170). Jesus did it all; there is nothing we can do. We come to Holy Communion not to accomplish anything, but to receive what has already been accomplished.

Devotional Context

In the Jerusalem temple, the place of God's presence was embodied in the temple "Holy of Holies," or sanctuary, which was set off by a curtain. In the performance of his duties as high priest, Jesus went into the presence of God. Jesus "passed through the heavens" (Hebrews 4:14) and entered "the inner shrine behind the curtain" (Hebrews 6:19). Entering the shrine behind the curtain, Jesus was "a forerunner on our behalf" (Hebrews 6:20)—as we now can follow into God's very presence.

The Gospel of Matthew says that at the time of Jesus' last breath, "the curtain of the temple was torn in two, from top to bottom" (Matthew 27:51). The barrier between the Holy of Holies and the rest of the temple—indeed, the rest of the world—was torn open. The curtain between heaven and earth, between God and humans, was no more. Jesus mediated a new covenant in which human beings have direct access to God.

SESSION THREE

Facilitator's Prayer

Gracious and loving God, in Jesus Christ you accomplished our salvation. Thank you. By your Spirit, strengthen my trust in the promise of your salvation for me. In all things, help me to rely on Jesus as my example and guide. When I fall or fail, as I inevitably will, help me joyfully to rely on Jesus' faith and obedience and your promise to use even my shortcomings for your purpose. Amen.

Gather (10-15 minutes)

Check-in

Invite learners to share completed homework or any new thoughts or insights about the last session. Be ready to give a brief recap of that session if necessary.

Pray

Lord Jesus, we gather here today because of you, who have called us together to study your Word. Open our hearts and minds, our eyes and ears to new understanding of who you are and of what you have done for the whole world, including us, each and every one. Amen.

Focus Activity

As a group, brainstorm a list of descriptive words and titles for Jesus.

Tip: List words and titles on a whiteboard or chart paper, then note whether "high priest" is on the group's list.

Tip: Few, if any, participants will be familiar with the image of Jesus as high priest, though some have likely seen images of Jesus in that role. Note that we commonly use the term "pastor," while in Hebrew tradition—and for Martin Luther as well—the term is "priest."

Open Scripture (10-15 minutes)

The texts for this session are divided into three portions. Form three groups and have each one read and present one portion of text to the group as a whole.

OR

Set a lighted candle, a chalice, and a paten in the midst of your group as participants take turns reading aloud. *Before lighting candles, check your local fire codes and your congregation's fire policies regarding the use of open flames.*

Read Hebrews 4:14—5:10; 9:24—10:1; 10:10-18.
- What word, phrases, or images stand out to you?
- What questions do you have?
- What, if anything, is confusing or troubling?

SESSION THREE

The texts for this session are long and somewhat technical. They will raise many questions—more than can be covered in this session. The elaboration of this session's texts in Hebrews 7 and 8 and other portions of Hebrews 9 and 10 will help in some ways and raise other questions as well. Some of the Enrichment activities are designed to respond to questions that may arise.

Join the Conversation (25-55 minutes)
Historical Context

1. In biblical times, the temple in Jerusalem was the center of Jewish faith. Within the temple, the "Holy of Holies" was seen as the place of God's presence. Only the high priest entered the Holy of Holies and only once a year.

- Compare the layout of the temple (see the diagram below) with the layout of your congregation's worship space, noting the similarities and differences. What questions does this comparison raise?

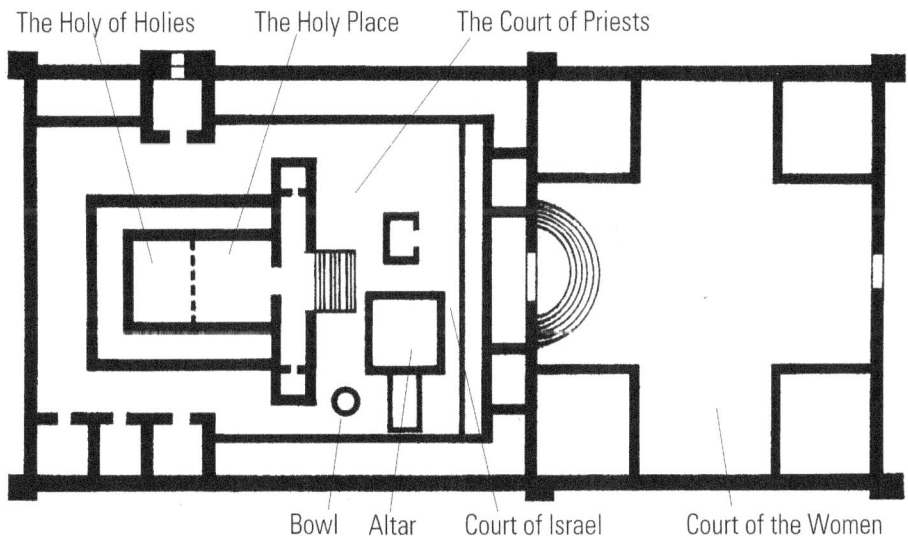

The Interior of the Temple in Jerusalem, New Testament Times. © 2009 Augsburg Fortress

 Bonus Activity:
Take the group into your congregation's worship space. Some participants may be very familiar with the entire space. Others may find those spaces intimidating. Walk around the entire space. Talk about how each area functions in worship and in the life of the congregation. If people are, for example, behind the table for the first time or at the font for the first time, ask them to share how it feels. (This activity may not fit for some contemporary worship spaces that are not as structured or separated as more traditional spaces.)

Session 3: Hebrews 4:14—5:10; 9:24—10:1; 10:10-18

SESSION THREE

2. In Jewish faith and tradition, the primary role of priests was to serve God. Priests were intermediaries, who spoke to God on behalf of the people and to the people on behalf of God. Some, notably the high priest, served God at the community's primary site of worship (the Jerusalem temple, while it was standing). The high priest played a particularly important role in the community's annual rite of sacrifice and renewal. This rite brought *atonement*—the restoration of the broken relationship between God and sinful humans. On the Day of Atonement, the priest entered the Holy of Holies and made sacrifices to atone for his own sins and the sins of all the people.

Tip:
Keep in mind that the biblical text's description of the Day of Atonement is an ancient ideal.

- The Day of Atonement or, in Hebrew, Yom Kippur, is described in Leviticus 16–17. Scan these chapters and summarize the work of the high priest Aaron.
- Scan Hebrews 4:14—5:10; 9:24—10:1; and 10:10-18, and summarize the work of the high priests.

Literary Context

1. Christology is the area in theology that studies the person and work of Jesus Christ. It is also a major theme in Hebrews.

- Find out what Hebrews says about the person and work of Jesus Christ by scanning Hebrews 4:14—5:10; 9:24—10:1; and 10:10-18. List the comparisons made of Jesus to other priests, of Jesus' work to the work of others, and of Jesus' sacrifice to other sacrifices.
- Summarize what these comparisons say about the person and work of Jesus Christ. What did Jesus do in a physical sense? What did Jesus do in himself? What did Jesus do on earth? What did Jesus do in heaven?

Tip:
The writer of Hebrews gives the original readers a philosophical perspective on Jesus' place in their religious traditions, again contrasting one thing against another as in Greek thought of the time. The contrast of Jesus' high priesthood with the traditional priesthood relies on these dichotomies.

2. Hebrews likens Jesus to the Old Testament figure Melchizedek, who is only referred to twice outside Hebrews.

- Read Genesis 14:17-20; Psalm 110:4; and Hebrews 7, and list the similarities and differences between Jesus and Melchizedek.
- What do these comparisons say about the person and work of Jesus Christ?

Bonus Activity:
Form two groups and move to distinct areas of the room, where all are still visible to one another. Assign one group to be the earthly group; the other, the heavenly group. Then, alternating between the two groups, ask each group to pose or dance in response to the following paired words or phrases: earth/heaven, incomplete/perfect, mortal/immortal, many/one, temporary/eternal, sinful/blameless, copy/original, changing/permanent, again and again/once and for all, and shadow/reality.

Lutheran Context

1. Lutherans focus on God's actions, rather than our own. Martin Luther writes that Jesus "makes useless absolutely all the righteousness and deeds of penitence. . . . Before we repent, our sins have already been forgiven" (Lectures on Hebrews, *Luther's Works* 29:112).

- How do you react to Luther's statement? List the feelings and questions it raises for you.
- Review the session Scripture texts. How do they support Luther's statement?

2. In Hebrews' terms, as high priest, Jesus made atonement for all our sins once and for all. For Luther, this is the heart of the gospel, that our sins are forgiven. Jesus accomplished this work on the cross, when he said, "It is finished" (John 19:30). On the cross Jesus offered himself for our sake—and was exalted.

- Luther emphasized the importance of believing not only that Jesus did this work for us, but that Jesus did this work for you. Salvation is *for you*.
- Reflect on the Focus Image and on Jesus' work as high priest and as complete sacrifice. Then describe in words or drawings what Jesus did for you and how you feel about this.

Devotional Context

1. Hebrews uses the image of Jesus as Great High Priest. Make a list of ways you picture Jesus. Do you include high priest on your list? Why or why not?

2. Hebrews 4:16 says, "Approach the throne of grace with boldness." Be bold in your prayers to God. Take time for silence to consider things you may want to say, but feel aren't quite appropriate for prayer. For example, if there's something you're embarrassed to be thankful for, thank God for that thing. If you're angry with God about something, let God know it. If you are hiding something (even from yourself a bit), tell it. If you just don't understand something, ask for an explanation.

Bonus Activity:

Have each participant choose a set of words to depict in a drawing. The words for Set 1 are *earth, incomplete, mortal, many, temporary, sinful, copy, changing, again and again*, and *shadow*. Set 2 words are *heaven, perfect, immortal, one, eternal, blameless, original, permanent, once and for all*, and *reality*. After a time—some people will be finished and others not—ask participants, as they are comfortable, to share their drawings and any comments they wish to make about what they drew.

Bonus Activity:

Participants may have experiences from varied Christian congregations and denominations and non-Christian faith traditions. Ask participants to share their experiences of what different traditions teach about Jesus—who he is, what he did, and his role in daily life. The conversation may surface some differences, not only in past experience but also in current understanding. As in other instances, you needn't resolve these differences. It's enriching for people to learn about the diversity in their experiences and backgrounds.

Tip:

Participants will have varied perspectives on Holy Communion—its importance, meaning, and practice. Jesus' "sacrifice" being the basis of communion may be a horror to some and commonplace to others. Hebrews is very strong on the role of sacrifice in salvation, but the issue is debated: Was Jesus' death a sacrifice? Is the Eucharist a sacrifice? You don't need to answer these hard questions. An Enrichment activity and a suggested reading help to address them.

SESSION THREE

Bonus Activity:
Participants may wonder why a loving God would require the death of Jesus. Was Jesus' death a sacrifice, as Hebrews frames it? Did God require it? Or, was it the consequence of human sinfulness? If so, what does it mean that God, rather than requiring atonement (another sacrifice) for this sin, responds with forgiveness and resurrection? What does it mean that Jesus the high priest is also the sacrifice? Engage participants in these questions, noting that Christians have wrestled with them for centuries.

Tip:
If a pastor is present, consider celebrating Holy Communion as part of your closing. If this isn't practical, sharing food—before, during, or after your session—is always a powerful way to draw people together.

Tip:
Make sure everyone feels welcome to be part of the group and its activities. For extra activities the group plans together, such as attending Holy Communion or a synagogue service, be sure to invite all participants. Keep this in mind not only for study-related activities, but also for more informal or spontaneous activities, such as going out for snacks or a meal together before or after a session.

3. In Jesus Christ, we know God in flesh. In Jesus' work of salvation, he gave us direct access to God. Close your eyes and visualize a time or place where you experienced God's presence. Meditate on that experience. Savor it. Let yourself rest in it.

Wrap-up

1. If there are any questions to explore further, write them on chart paper or a whiteboard. Ask for volunteers to do further research to share with the group at the next session.

2. Solicit, and record for all to see, responses to the question, "What did Jesus do?" Among the variety of responses, be sure ways of saying the following are included: obeyed, suffered and died, offered (or sacrificed) himself, removed sin once and for all (and for *me*), abolished the old law and established the new, perfected those who are sanctified (including *me*), and, from the previous session, destroyed the devil and the power of death (Hebrews 2:14) and perfected salvation (Hebrews 2:10). In the next session, you will read that Jesus also pioneered and perfected faith (Hebrews 12:2).

3. Ask participants to share a hymn title or line or another quotation or idiom that expresses what Jesus did.

Pray

Pray or sing together "Now Thank We All Our God" (*LBW* 533, 534; *ELW* 839, 840).

Extending the Conversation (5 minutes)

Homework

1. Read the next session's Bible text: Hebrews 11:1-40.

2. Attend worship with other members of your study group. Be mindful that we come to Holy Communion not to accomplish anything, but to receive and celebrate what has already been accomplished for us by God's grace—the forgiveness of all our sins in Jesus Christ. Following worship, take some time together to reflect on the experience.

3. Philippians 2:5-11 is an ancient confessional hymn about the person and work of Jesus Christ. Slowly read the words of this text aloud each day, taking time to hear the words as you speak them.

4. You have explored the work of Jesus Christ—and what Jesus has done for you. How would you describe that to someone else? Practice sharing what you would say about this to someone in your "comfort zone"—a member of your study group, church, or family, or a friend. When opportunities arise, consider sharing within and beyond your normal comfort zone.

Enrichment

1. If you want to read through the entire book of Hebrews during this unit, read the following sections this week.
Day 1: Hebrews 6:13-20
Day 2: Hebrews 7:1-10
Day 3: Hebrews 7:11-19
Day 4: Hebrews 7:20-28
Day 5: Hebrews 8:1-7
Day 6: Hebrews 8:8-13
Day 7: Hebrews 9:1-10

2. As a group, invite a rabbi to meet with you to talk about contemporary Yom Kippur observance, as well as other traditions referred to in Hebrews. If your pastor and the rabbi are willing, ask them to talk with your group about Jewish-Christian relations.

3. As a group or individually with a friend or acquaintance, attend a synagogue service. Take time following the service to debrief with one another and your host. How does the service compare to worship services you're used to? What surprised you? If portions of the service are in Hebrew, what was that like for you?

4. The Jerusalem temple has an important history, some of which is reflected in the Gospels. Particularly if you're a history buff, an architect, or interested in archaeology, you'll find it interesting. You can start with what the Bible has to say about the temple—from its architectural specifications to its use and abuse. From there, go online to see drawings of what the temple—really a series of structures—may have been like and to learn about its intriguing religious, theological, cultural, and political history.

SESSION THREE

For Further Reading

Available from augsburgfortress.org:

Fortress Introduction to Salvation and the Cross by David A. Brondos (Minneapolis: Fortress Press, 2007).

Holy Things: A Liturgical Theology by Gordon Lathrop (Minneapolis: Fortress Press, 1993). See especially chapter 6, "The Christian Sacrifice," pp. 139–58.

Looking Ahead

1. Read the next session's Bible text: Hebrews 11:1-40.

2. Read through the Leader Guide for the next session and mark portions you wish to highlight for the group.

3. Make a checklist of any materials you'll need to do the Bonus Activities.

4. Pray for members of your group during the week.

SESSION FOUR

Hebrews 11:1-40

Leader Session Guide

Focus Statement

Faith is hearing God's word with our whole lives—obeying God's promises in hopeful and expectant trust, despite appearances. The countless people who have gone before us and lived by faith are models and inspiration for us.

Key Verse

Now faith is the assurance of things hoped for, the conviction of things not seen. Indeed, by faith our ancestors received approval. By faith we understand that the worlds were prepared by the word of God, so that what is seen was made from things that are not visible. Hebrews 11:1-3

Focus Image

© Design Pics / SuperStock

What Is Faith?

Session Preparation

Before You Begin . . .

Faith is a gift from God. When and from whom did you first receive the gift of faith? Take a moment to reflect on that relationship and to give thanks. Close your eyes for a moment and picture one by one the individuals or groups that have sustained you in faith.

Session Instructions

1. Read this Session Guide completely and highlight or underline any portions you wish to emphasize with the group. Note any Bonus Activities you wish to do.

2. If you plan to do any special activities, check to see what materials you'll need, if any.

3. Have extra Bibles on hand in case a member of the group forgets to bring one.

Session Overview

The litany of chapter 11 provides models of faith and inspiration to believers. Faith is living on promises of realities not yet seen. Faith is hearing God's Word with our entire being and obeying the promises. Faith is persevering in the face of challenge, following the pioneer Jesus, and relying on Jesus' complete faith when ours is incomplete.

HISTORICAL CONTEXT

Within a Jewish community of the first century, this roll call of the faithful in Hebrews 11 would have evoked history and legends told and retold in community rituals and education.

Stories of early forebears in faith are found in Genesis roughly as follows: Cain and Abel, sons of Adam and Eve (4:1-16); Enoch, who "walked with God" (5:22-24); Noah (6:9—9:19); Abraham and Sarah (12-23); and their descendants Isaac, Jacob, and Joseph (24-50).

Joseph's story continues in Exodus, along with the stories of Moses and Aaron, about whom we read through Deuteronomy. The Historical Books of the Bible contain many stories of exemplars in faith: Rahab (Joshua 2), Barak (Judges 4-5), Gideon (Judges 6-8), Jephthah (Judges 11-12), Samson (Judges 13-16), Samuel (1 Samuel 1-12), and David (1 and 2 Samuel).

SESSION FOUR

Hebrews 11:33-38 refers to others, although not by name: Daniel in the lions' den (Daniel 6); the three youths in the fiery furnace (Daniel 3); the woman of Zarephath, whose son the prophet Elijah revived (1 Kings 17:17-24); the Shunammite woman, whose son the prophet Elisha revived (2 Kings 4:25-37); Zechariah, who was stoned to death for prophesying (2 Chronicles 24:20-22); and the prophet Uriah, who was killed by King Jehoiakim with a sword (Jeremiah 26:20-23).

The readers of the letter to the Hebrews have a long line of forebears and exemplars to uphold them. Believers need to rely on these witnesses amid trials that are sure to come. What these witnesses did not see and know, the readers of Hebrews know in Jesus Christ, who perfected the faith of the forebears as well as that of current believers.

LITERARY CONTEXT

Hebrews 11 is a genealogy of faith. Each name and event evokes a rich set of associations—stories, characters, places, and hardships overcome. These comprise a history of what God has done and what God will do.

Faith is hopeful and expectant trust in God's promises, despite appearances. The **assurance** of things hoped for is the reality in the present of God's promise for the future. The genealogy of faith tells of those who, with the eyes of faith, acted on the reality of the future without seeing its fulfillment.

Notice the many times the word *faith* is used in Hebrews 11. The people named share faith. They act on "things not seen," "unseen," and "not visible." They act "not knowing" where God's call will lead and look forward to the fulfillment of God's promises.

Place is important in the people's responses to God's promises. Abraham sets out for "a place," not knowing where he is going, and lives for a time in "a foreign land." These forebears anticipate "a city," a better "country," a "homeland." They leave behind what they know for what they don't know. In this way, the writer associates faith with what we'd call risk-taking.

? Assurance:

The Greek word *hypostasis*, translated as "assurance" in Hebrews 11:1 in the NRSV, is the same word used in the Nicene Creed when it says that Jesus is "of one *being* with the Father." *Hypostasis* is sometimes translated in Hebrews 11:1 as "substance" (King James Version and New English Bible) and "reality" (Harold W. Attridge, *Hebrews*, Hermeneia [Minneapolis: Fortress Press, 1989], p. 307; see also Luther's reference to Chrysostom, *Luther's Works* 29:230). The intent is to say that faith is the present reality of the future promise.

The author—like Martin Luther—reads the Old Testament as foreshadowing Jesus Christ. The witness and perseverance of faithful people point to the expectation of promises fulfilled in Jesus.

LUTHERAN CONTEXT

Faith is a gift we receive through God's Word. Faith is obedience. Martin Luther's understanding of *obedience* was based on its root meaning in Hebrew and Greek (as in English): obedience is to hear. This is not about obeying rules or laws. It is about obeying God's promise, the future God has spoken. Relying on God's promise, faith sees what is not seen.

You turn unthinking when you hear your name called. Your attention leaves what you're doing when you hear the ring of the phone. This is obedience—hearing and responding. Disobedience would be hearing the sound and reserving any response.

Abraham's faith was his obeying God's promise. Abraham "went out with no knowledge of where he was going, with nothing for him to follow except the Word of God concerning things which were nowhere to be seen.... And this is the glory of faith, ... to follow the bare voice of God and to be led and driven rather than to drive" (*Luther's Works* 29:238).

This faith—utter reliance on God's promises alone—is what Luther is talking about in his teaching on **justification**, his central understanding of the gospel. The Lutheran doctrine of justification is this: we are made righteous before God—saved—by God's grace alone in Jesus Christ alone through faith alone, apart from any works, anything we might do.

DEVOTIONAL CONTEXT

Grounded in and responding to God's promise, faith has an inherent orientation toward the future. Looking back on the history of God's promises and on God's actions, faith anticipates God's own faithfulness in fulfilling promises and continuing to be God. The future is not without surprises. Yet, we know what the future is like: justice, peace, and freedom, all people eating together, all creation reconciled and made whole. We know this future from the past. We know this future in God's Word, which is God's promise. We know this future in Jesus Christ—Jesus' life, suffering, death, and resurrection.

 Justification:
Justification is being made just or righteous with God. For Luther, the central teaching of the gospel was salvation by grace alone through faith alone for Christ's sake alone. Justification is entirely God's doing in Jesus Christ. Our true righteousness comes from outside ourselves. As Christ is the perfecter of our faith, so Christ is the perfecter of our righteousness.

SESSION FOUR

The Cotton Patch Version of Hebrews is a paraphrase by Clarence Jordan. Jordan begins Hebrews 11 this way: "Now faith is turning dreams into deeds; it is betting your life on the unseen realities" (*The Cotton Patch Version of Hebrews and the General Epistles: A Colloquial Translation with a Southern Accent*, New York: Association Press, 1973).

Sometimes it feels frightening or seems foolish to "dream" of the promises of God fulfilled—peace on earth, all people together. Faith lives as if these are not only guaranteed but also already real—because they are in God's Word. This doesn't mean people become perfect. It does mean learning to rely on God's grace and the promise that that future is *the* future.

Facilitator's Prayer

Gracious and loving God, we who will gather for this study are inheritors from a great line of your faithful people. As we learn more about our inheritance of faith, help us to be grateful for those who have gone before—and make us worthy by your grace to stand among them. As I lead this session, complete my faith, dear Jesus, that it may be an encouragement to others. I pray by the power of your life-giving Spirit. Amen.

Gather (10-15 minutes)

Check-in

Invite learners to share completed homework or any new thoughts or insights about the last session. Be ready to give a brief recap of that session if necessary.

Tip: Especially if some, but not all, members of the group attended worship together as part of the homework, take a few moments for those who attended to tell the entire group about that experience. If everyone did attend worship together, encourage all to take part in debriefing the experience as they feel comfortable.

Pray

Draw your church together, O God, into one great company of disciples, together following our teacher Jesus Christ into every walk of life, together serving in Christ's mission to the world, and together witnessing to your love wherever you will send us; for the sake of Jesus Christ our Lord. Amen. (*ELW*, p. 75)

Focus Activity

Get comfortable. Close your eyes and recall someone you would describe as a person of faith. What is it about the person that makes that description appropriate? What feelings do you have about the person? Describe this person's life, relationships, and speech. What do you recognize as faith?

Tip: Have participants form a line and join hands. Designate a person at one end of the line as the leader. Ask a volunteer to read the prayer aloud slowly, repeating it, if necessary. As the prayer is led, ask the leader to help everyone form a circle, with the people at the beginning and end of the line now joining hands. At the end of the prayer, stand quietly in the circle for a moment.

SESSION FOUR

Open Scripture (10-15 minutes)

Read Hebrews 11:1-3 aloud to the group. Then ask participants to take turns reading portions of the rest of the session Scripture text, dividing it according to the stories. (In Hebrews 11:4-31, have participants use the words "by faith" to signal a change of reader.) Divide Hebrews 11:32-40 between a "narrator" (Hebrews 11:32, 39-40) and readers taking one verse each (Hebrews 11:33-38).

Set up a series of illustrations and photos that are based on this text. (See www.textweek.com for a good starting point.) Display the illustrations and photos around the room and invite learners to walk through this "gallery" as you slowly read the Bible passage a few times.

Read Hebrews 11:1-40.

- What in the text touched you?
- What images stood out for you?
- What surprised you?

Join the Conversation (25-55 minutes)

Historical Context

1. God has provided many other exemplars of faith throughout history. For the original readers of Hebrews, in a Jewish community of the first century, the list of people in Hebrews 11 would have constituted a "roll call" of the faithful.

- What names are on your "roll call" of faithful people? Share the names and stories of some who are important to you. (They may be widely known; they may be known only to you.) How does sharing these names and stories affect you? Place the names on a timeline, according to the approximate dates of when each person lived.
- List the names of people included in Hebrews 11. How do you suppose the original readers of Hebrews were affected by this list of names?

 Tip: Learners may vary in their knowledge of the references in the lesson. A new Christian might be particularly in the dark. A Jewish Christian or former Jew among you may be quite knowledgeable. Affirm the knowledge of those who have lots of background without suggesting that lack of knowledge is a problem: people are participating to learn. Be particularly careful of any suggestion that one's measure of knowledge necessarily corresponds to one's measure of faith.

SESSION FOUR

Bonus Activity:

Moses is another key figure in the list of the faithful in Hebrews 11. Have volunteers read aloud Exodus 3:7—4:17. Ask participants to discuss briefly what is going on in the relationship between God and Moses. Then ask for two volunteers to role-play the negotiation that goes on between God and Moses about God sending Moses to bring the people out of slavery.

Bonus Activity:

Two women—Sarah and Rahab—are included in Hebrews' list of the faithful. Participants may be somewhat familiar with Sarah, Abraham's wife, but not so familiar with Rahab. Rahab's story is in Joshua 2:1-24 and 6:17-25. Ask volunteers to read the text aloud, taking the roles of narrator, Joshua, the spies, the king, and Rahab. (In preparation for this activity, make copies of the text and highlight the parts for readers.) Then have readers describe how they felt in their various roles. In the group as a whole, discuss why Rahab is included as one of the faithful.

Tip:

Some participants may react strongly to the idea of faith and *obedience*. They may feel that talk of obedience introduces works righteousness. Help distinguish obedience—truly hearing God's Word with our whole selves—from works righteousness, believing and acting as if we can save ourselves by what we do. Be mindful that for some, obedience has been an enriching experience; for others, obedience may have been learned in the context of an abusive relationship.

Bonus Activity:

Have ready copies of several translations of Hebrews 11:1-3. (You might include a paraphrase as well. Including the King James Version among the translations might be particularly helpful for people who used that version in their youth.) Compare the different versions. What insights do the similarities and contrasts provide?

2. The faithful people listed in Hebrews 11 obeyed God's promises in hopeful and expectant trust, despite appearances.

- Form two groups, one to read about Noah in Genesis 6:13-14, 17-19, and the other to read about Abraham in Genesis 12:1-3 and 15:1-6. Report back to the large group on these questions: What did God ask this person to do? What did God promise? Putting yourself in Noah's or Abraham's position, how would you feel about God's proposition to you? What would you take into consideration before agreeing to what God asked of you? Would you do it? Why or why not?

Literary Context

1. The Greek word *hypostasis*, translated as "assurance" in Hebrews 11:1, also appears in Hebrews 1:3 and 3:14. In those places, it is translated as "very being" and as "confidence" (NRSV). It has also been translated as "substance" (King James Version and New English Bible) and "reality" (Harold W. Attridge, *Hebrews*, Hermeneia [Minneapolis: Fortress Press, 1989], p. 307). It is the same word used in the Nicene Creed to say that Jesus is "of one *being* with the Father."

- How does this affect your reading of Hebrews 11:1-3? Read that passage again, and then put it in your own words.

2. Reflect on the Focus Image for a few moments. Then, in a group of three or four, come up with a way to tell others what faith is. Feel free to use a description, a simile (faith is like . . .), a story, a drawing, a pantomime, or some other medium.

Lutheran Context

1. Martin Luther writes, "Faith is God's work in us, that changes us and gives new birth from God. . . . It . . . makes us completely different people. It changes our hearts, our spirits, our thoughts and all our powers. It brings the Holy Spirit with it" ("Martin Luther's Definition of Faith: An excerpt from 'An Introduction to St. Paul's Letter to the Romans,'" tr. Robert E. Smith, Project Wittenberg, 1994).

- Read the quotation two more times. First, read it and list the *subjective* changes—changes we can feel or sense. Second, read the quotation and list the *objective* changes—changes that are real apart from what we might feel or sense. What difference do these two readings make in your image of what faith is?

2. Luther was emphatic that faith must precede good works. Works that proceed from faith are righteous. They rely on Christ's righteousness alone, Christ having perfected faith and sanctified believers. Works that precede faith rely on the person performing them. However good the works may be, they are a judgment on the person, who acts on his or her own righteousness, which cannot make the work itself or the person complete.

- What do you think about this? How would you describe the connection between faith and good works?

Devotional Context

1. Explore the nature of your faith. First, list three to five words that would be part of a description of your faith. Second, close your eyes and visualize your faith—what does your faith look like? Third, think of one reason why faith is important. Fourth, if you can, think of a piece of music—a hymn, a song, an instrumental tune, etc.—that somehow embodies what your faith is like. Finally, assume a pose that might convey your faith to someone looking at you.

2. Grounded in and responding to God's promise, faith has an inherent orientation toward the future. Looking back on the history of God's promises and on God's actions, faith anticipates God's own faithfulness in fulfilling promises and continuing to be God. The future is not without surprises. Yet, we know what the future is like: justice, peace, and freedom; all people eating together; all creation reconciled and made whole. We know this future from the past. We know this future in God's Word, which is God's promise. We know this future in Jesus Christ—Jesus' life, suffering, death, and resurrection.

Bonus Activity:

Review the session Scripture text. What words or phrases in the text suggest risk? What words or phrases suggest comfort? Overall, which does the text emphasize more—risk or comfort? Discuss what this might mean for a life of faith.

Bonus Activity:

Obtain a copy of *The Book of Concord* (Minneapolis: Fortress Press, 2000) and make copies of The Augsburg Confession, Article IV (pp. 38-41) and of the Smalcald Articles II (pp. 300-301). These passages focus on the "office and work of Jesus Christ." They are among the primary texts that focus on Lutheran teaching regarding justification. Ask participants to read them together. Discuss: What stands out? What is surprising? What questions do these texts raise? (The idea that justification is not something we accomplish, but that Christ alone accomplishes, may be disturbing to some. Take time to hear out any expressions of comfort, concern, or even anger.)

Bonus Activity:

Arrange ahead of time for a good singer—perhaps from the group, perhaps not—to prepare *LBW* 385, "What Wondrous Love Is This." Its origin unknown, the hymn was first published in 1843 in a collection called *Southern Harmony*. Dim the room lights and light a candle, if possible, to focus the group. Encourage participants to become comfortable and quiet. Ask them to close their eyes and listen while the hymn is sung. *Before lighting candles, check your local fire codes and your congregation's fire policies regarding the use of open flames.*

Session 4: Hebrews 11:1-40

SESSION FOUR

 Bonus Activity:
When we retell our faith forebears' stories, they become stories of our experience, too. We learn the hardships of the ancient people of God in Egypt. We learn the courage of those who stepped out, not knowing where they were going. "Lift Every Voice and Sing" (*ELW* 841, *This Far by Faith* 296) is a hymn of remembering history in ourselves today. Sing the hymn together.

 Bonus Activity:
Julie Gold wrote the song "From a Distance" in 1985. It's about the difference between how things seem and how they really are. Obtain a recording of the song and have participants listen quietly as the song is played. How does seeing things from God's perspective—as they really are—affect their feelings about themselves, other people, and the world?

 Tip:
People vary in their approach to faith. For most people, faith relies on a combination of four dimensions: Scripture, reason, experience, and tradition. Different people will emphasize different dimensions and in differing proportions. Noting these different ways of understanding will help participants be open to one another's ways of faith.

- Imagine the future. First, consider Abraham and Sarah and the future in which they trusted: a promised land, a heavenly country, a child born in their old age. Consider their wandering in unknown territory not knowing where they were going, much less the way there. They met obstacles as well as opportunities.
- Now, in your mind's eye or on paper, envision your future—the promises of God fulfilled for you. What does it look like?

Wrap-up

1. If there are any questions to explore further, write them on chart paper or a whiteboard. Ask for volunteers to do further research to share with the group at the next session.

2. Ask participants to call out quickly words or images that are important in understanding what faith is.

3. Have participants read aloud together Hebrews 11:1-3.

Pray

Thank you for all those who, through the ages and in my own life, have witnessed to your love and faithfulness, to your justice and mercy. Make us such witnesses that our faith might help others to know your lovingkindness and faithfulness to all people and all creation. As we go about our lives in the coming days, let the light of our faith shine before others that they may see how we live and glorify you. Amen.

Extending the Conversation (5 minutes)

Homework

1. Read the next session's Bible text: Hebrews 12:1-17; 13:1-19.

2. This week as you go about your daily life, be mindful of the people you encounter whose faith examples are important to you. Take a moment to pray a word of thanks for them. If you are able and comfortable doing it, let these people know about your gratitude for their faith. As you express your thanks in person or in a note, give a concrete example of what you mean.

3. Faith grows by passing it on. It grows by contagion and it grows in the person who passes it on. Tell the story of someone whose faith has been an example to you. (If you would prefer, try writing or recording the story.) Tell a little about the person, the person's faith, and how it has affected you. If you are a parent, you might tell your child. You might tell another member of your family or a friend. Perhaps you might tell a coworker or neighbor. Surprisingly, you might find yourself telling the story in a conversation with a virtual stranger.

Tip:
To encourage and support participants in Homework activity #3, be prepared to tell a story of someone whose faith has been an example to you and how it has affected you. Your account needn't be long or complicated. The more straightforward your story, the better model it will be for others.

Enrichment

1. If you want to read through the entire book of Hebrews during this unit, read the following sections this week.
Day 1: Hebrews 9:11-14
Day 2: Hebrews 9:15-22
Day 3: Hebrews 9:23-28
Day 4: Hebrews 10:1-10
Day 5: Hebrews 10:11-18
Day 6: Hebrews 10:19-25
Day 7: Hebrews 10:26-39

2. Daily life carries images for our faith. What are your regular activities? Focus on one—cooking, typing, driving, teaching, running, filing, caring for a parent or child, cutting hair, knitting, wiring houses, waiting tables, preparing legal briefs, playing basketball. What are the individual actions that make up the whole? Is there an action that you can see as an image related to faith? For example, wait staff serve others, electricians provide light and energy for people's lives, office workers create order amid chaos. Begin with that single connection and gradually reflect on the entire activity, making other connections to faith.

3. Organize a faith-focused reading group. Particularly if people are busy, try using *A Celestial Omnibus: Short Fiction on Faith*, ed. J. P. Maney and Tom Hazuka (Boston: Beacon Press, 1998).

For Further Reading

Dynamics of Faith by Paul Tillich (New York: HarperOne, 2001).

Murder in the Cathedral by T. S. Eliot (New York: Harcourt Brace, 1963).

SESSION FOUR

Looking Ahead

1. Read the next session's Bible text: Hebrews 12:1-17; 13:1-19.

2. Read through the Leader Guide for the next session and mark portions you wish to highlight for the group.

3. Make a checklist of any materials you'll need to do the Bonus Activities.

4. Pray for members of your group during the week.

SESSION FIVE

Hebrews 12:1-17; 13:1-19

Leader Session Guide

Focus Statement

Jesus has perfected our faith. We can lay aside sin, which no longer binds us, and follow where Jesus has pioneered the way. Faith practices, like athletic practice, are part of how we condition ourselves for lives of following.

Key Verse

Therefore, since we are surrounded by so great a cloud of witnesses, let us also lay aside every weight and the sin that clings so closely and let us run with perseverance the race that is set before us, looking to Jesus the pioneer and perfecter of our faith.
Hebrews 12:1-2a

Focus Image

© OJO Images / SuperStock

How Shall We Live?

Session Preparation

Before You Begin . . .

You have persevered, now, into the fifth of six sessions! No doubt, you feel good about some moments in the sessions and not so good about others. Give God the glory for all that's been and will be good from your efforts. Be confident that where you may have fallen short, Jesus the pioneer and perfecter of our faith will make things whole and useful in ways that you cannot imagine.

Session Instructions

1. Read this Session Guide completely and highlight or underline any portions you wish to emphasize with the group. Note any Bonus Activities you wish to do.

2. If you plan to do any special activities, check to see what materials you'll need, if any.

3. Have extra Bibles on hand in case a member of the group forgets to bring one.

4. You may want to visit the ELCA Web site to learn more about faith practices. This session presents an opportunity for you to encourage participants to do the same.

Session Overview

Jesus has pioneered a way of life for us. We live our lives utterly dependent on Jesus to perfect our faith and to make our efforts whole. We live pursuing peace, caring for others, showing love and hospitality, being faithful, not being distracted by money, doing good, and respecting witnesses to the gospel who, with Jesus, show us the way.

HISTORICAL CONTEXT

We don't know the exact circumstances or history of Hebrews' original audience. The letter suggests that at least some of the readers have experienced firsthand persecution—imprisonment and torture. The letter also indicates that during that time the faith of the people was vibrant and active. In easier times, however, it appears that people began to take faith for granted and became lax and indifferent.

SESSION FIVE

The church has known persecution throughout its history. After Jesus' torture and execution, Jesus' followers were subject to the same threat. The book of Acts recounts Peter and John's arrest, Stephen's stoning, persecution in Jerusalem, Paul and Silas' imprisonment, and Paul's later arrest and beating. Some religious persecution was carried out within the Jewish community in the struggle over the Jesus movement, viewed by some to be heretical. However, the Roman Empire had the might and resources to be the primary source of persecution, beginning under Nero.

LITERARY CONTEXT

Hebrews 12 contains an extended athletic metaphor: run the race, perseverance, discipline, body images, endurance. The Greek word translated as *witness* can also mean *spectator*. We, who run the race, are surrounded by a crowd cheering us on! Read the preparations of 12:1 as preparations for the race, which requires endurance and discipline. It is more like a marathon than a 50-meter dash. Jesus not only inspires but teaches us to "not grow weary or lose heart" (Hebrews 12:3). **Discipline** refers not only to parental instruction, but also to athletic training.

> **? Discipline:**
> *Discipline* comes from the same root as *disciple*, which means "student." A follower of a particular philosophical or religious school is a disciple. While we commonly think of discipline in relationship to punishment, discipline is more accurately described as training, practice, or education. Disciplining a child is teaching the child. A well-disciplined person has—through training and exercise—a measure of self-control in doing something. One might learn the discipline of economics. Musicians exercise the discipline of daily practice. An athlete disciplines her body with training, which is sometimes painful.

The session Scripture texts include a variety of instructions—or teachings, disciplines—about relationships. Several make clear that believers are responsible for one another's spiritual well-being. Some refer to caring for others, regardless of whether we know the people or not. Note the pairing of mutual love with hospitality, of remembering prisoners with remembering torture victims (with whom believers are to identify especially, having suffered persecution themselves), and of sexuality and money. Early Christians understood lust and greed as incompatible with community life.

Remembrance and imitation are means of relating to and integrating the examples of our forebears in the faith, as well as of Jesus the pioneer of our faith.

LUTHERAN CONTEXT

During his career, Martin Luther became aware of a pitfall in his theology—the possibility that people would misunderstand justification as meaning they didn't have to do anything. Historically this misunderstanding resulted in a tight focus on faith rather than works within some Lutheran bodies.

Luther warned against the use of good works as a way to achieve salvation, and against good works without faith. He did teach, however, that good works or practices issue from faith. He wrote, "It is impossible for faith in [Christ] to be idle; for it is alive, and it itself works and triumphs, and in this way works flow forth spontaneously from faith. For in this way our patience flows from the patience of Christ, and our humility from His, and the other good works in like manner, provided that we believe firmly that He has done all these things for us, and not only for us but also before our eyes" (*Luther's Works* 29:123).

Devotional Context

When is there time for faith exercises and faith practices? Work crowds out adequate time with family and friends. It's hard to get to the gym on a regular basis. The chaos at home gets so bad, it's hard to know where to begin to create some order. The only quiet time many people get, if they're lucky, is on the way to and from work. More and more studies attest that most of us don't get enough sleep.

If there is not time for practicing faith, we lose track of our way of life (of which we will say more in the next session). More importantly for this session, carving out time with family and friends, caring for ourselves, beginning somewhere, taking quiet time, and resting adequately are part of the practice of faith. We are free to put first things first. We are free to "lay aside every weight and the sin that clings so closely, and [to] run with perseverance the race that is set before us" (Hebrews 12:1).

Facilitator's Prayer

O God, thank you for bringing us this far. Thank you for those who are persevering with me in our study. As I lead this session, I pray you give me grace to be an example, grace to teach and grace to learn, grace to speak and grace to listen, grace to give and grace to receive, grace to lead and grace to follow. In all of these, I rely on you alone. Amen.

Gather (10-15 minutes)

Check-in

Invite learners to share completed homework or any new thoughts or insights about the last session. Be ready to give a brief recap of that session if necessary.

SESSION FIVE

 Tip:
Have someone in the group read the Focus Activity aloud while the others close their eyes and visualize it. Be sure to take adequate time for this visualization. Coach the reader to go slowly and pause frequently, especially between images.

 Tip:
A paraphrase is not a direct translation. Both of these paraphrases put the text in lively and engaging contemporary English.

Pray

Gracious and loving God, we gather to be with you in your Word and with one another in you. Help us together to learn a way of life that not only sustains us in faith, but also witnesses to the great power of your love. As we gather here and always, keep us mindful of those who have not heard of your love, that we might learn boldness to proclaim in deed and word. Amen.

Focus Activity

Close your eyes and get comfortable. Imagine that you are on a path. A 500-pound (225 km) block is in your way. Try to move it. How does that feel? How does this affect your body? How does this affect your attitude? Slowly change your focus from the block to the path ahead. Jesus is walking toward you. When Jesus reaches the block, he picks it up and hurls it out of sight. He proceeds along the path, gesturing for you to come along.

Open Scripture (10-15 minutes)

As a volunteer reads the session Scripture texts, have participants underline any words or phrases that stand out to them or that they would like to know more about.

Read the texts from the New Revised Standard Version. Read them again from Clarence Jordan's paraphrase, *The Cotton Patch Version of Hebrews and the General Epistles: A Colloquial Translation with a Southern Accent* (New York: Association Press, 1973), or from Eugene H. Peterson's paraphrase of the New Testament, *The Message* (Colorado Springs: NavPress, 1993).

Read Hebrews 12:1-17; 13:1-19.
- In a word or phrase, what is your first reaction to these texts?
- What images stand out?
- What questions do you have?

50   Hebrews Leader Guide

Join the Conversation (25-55 minutes)
Historical Context

1. The church has known persecution throughout its history. After Jesus' torture and execution, Jesus' followers were subject to the same threat. The book of Acts tells of persecution including arrests, beatings, imprisonment, and stoning. Some religious persecution was carried out within the Jewish community in the struggle over the new "Jesus movement," viewed by some as heretical. The Roman Empire, however, had the might and resources to be the primary source of persecution, beginning under Nero.

- Review Hebrews 12:1-17 and 13:1-19, and list words or phrases indicating that the original readers of Hebrews may have experienced persecution for their faith.

2. Imagine yourself as one of the original readers of Hebrews. Sometime in the past, you and your faith community, and perhaps family members, were persecuted for your faith. Either your faith was active enough that you were a threat, or perhaps you or those you knew were treated as an example to put fear in believers. Make some notes about how you feel. Discuss how persecution might have affected your faith and the practice of your faith.

- The persecution of Jesus' followers subsides over time. The memories of persecution remain, but you and those you know are safer now. How does this feel? Discuss how this turn of events might affect your faith and the practice of your faith.

Bonus Activity:

Ask a volunteer to read aloud, as a parent reads a story, the account of Stephen's witness and persecution in Acts 6:8—7:60. Following the reading, observe a couple of minutes of silence. Then pray together for people of faith in every time and place who have suffered imprisonment, torture, or execution.

Bonus Activity:

Often people involved in new church development or missionary activity speak of the faith-enlivening nature of those ministries. If any members of your group have been part of a mission congregation, mission development, or missionary work, ask them to share their experiences. What kinds of challenges did they face? How did they deal with these challenges? What is the difference between being in a mission congregation and an established congregation?

SESSION FIVE

Tip:
Athletic metaphors were common in literature in biblical times. Physical beauty, as they defined it, and athletic skill were prized by ancient Greeks. Contemporary North American culture has its own version of this idealism. As you discuss the athletic and physical metaphors in this passage, be mindful of the varying physical abilities of members of the group.

Bonus Activity:
The apostle Paul also made use of athletic metaphors in his letters. Have participants read aloud and compare 1 Corinthians 9:24-27 and Philippians 3:12-16 with this session's text. What are the similarities and differences? What new insights come from considering these additional passages? (Depending on the size of your group and the time available, other texts to include are Galatians 2:2; Philippians 2:16; 2 Timothy 2:5; and 2 Timothy 4:7-8.)

Bonus Activity:
Just as the Bible uses athletic metaphors to talk about faith, sports reporters use theological metaphors to talk about athletics. Gather sports magazines and sports sections from newspapers. Form teams of three or four and have them scan the news items and advertisements for theological terms and references. For example, did a particular player "save" the day?

Bonus Activity:
Although we are saved by Christ alone, we are constantly tempted to try to save ourselves by what we do. Many of us practice works righteousness in our lives every day. Some of us who have the choice still overwork to secure our reputations, wealth, or position, to the neglect of our families, sleep, or worship. Some of us cling to the responsibility of saving another person when it is not in our power. In pairs, ask participants to share with one another a time—probably fairly recent—when they did something with at least a tinge of works righteousness. Invite them to discuss how acting in faith might have changed things.

Literary Context

1. In Hebrews 12:1-13, the writer uses imagery from an athletic contest to encourage readers to follow Jesus in faith.

- Scan Hebrews 12:1-13 and list words or phrases that refer to an athlete or athletic competition.
- Reflect on the Focus Image. In the "race" of faith, what does the "cloud of witnesses" do? What does Jesus do? What do we do?

2. Hebrews 12:12-13 says, "Lift your drooping hands and strengthen your weak knees, and make straight paths for your feet." To understand this image more fully, intentionally distort something about your posture. For example, let your hands droop, slouch, raise your shoulders to your ears (or put an ear to your shoulder), stand on one leg, or stick one hip out to the side. What does the rest of your body do in response? How do you compensate?

- Now return to your normal sitting or standing position. How does this feel? What does it do for your sense of self?

3. Portions of the session Scripture texts provide "instructions" for living as a follower of Jesus.
Read Hebrews 12:14-16 and 13:1-17, listing the instructions provided in these passages. Which ones seem most important? Which seem easier to do than others? Which, if any, are confusing or troubling? Are there any instructions that surprise you?

Lutheran Context

1. The primary lens through which Lutherans read Scripture is that of law and gospel. God's law is everything God asks of us. Because we cannot do all that God asks, we must look to God for grace, mercy, love, and forgiveness. The gospel is everything God does for us.

- Review the session Scripture texts. Underline words or phrases that you hear as law, and circle words or phrases that you hear as gospel. What effect does doing this have on you?

2. Hebrews 12–13 talks about how we should live. Yet we know that as sinners we are unable to do everything that God asks. No matter what we do, we cannot get everything right in our lives. What should we do, then, when we're uncertain about how to proceed, or must choose from options that all have problems or drawbacks? In a letter to his friend Philip Melanchthon, Martin Luther writes, "Be a sinner and sin boldly, but believe and rejoice in Christ even more boldly, for he is victorious over sin, death, and the world" (*Luther's Works* 48:282).

- What do you think Luther means by this advice? Tell about a time when you or someone you know acted or moved forward boldly in faith.
- Consider a dilemma you're facing. Describe or doodle your dilemma on a piece of paper. In what you've written or drawn, where is the focus of the unresolved issue? On that place, write the words, "I rejoice in Jesus Christ."

Devotional Context

1. Faith practices are actions that nurture the growth of faith. They are for every day, every moment, every place in our lives. Take a look at the ELCA's Faith Practices Wheel (below). Several faith practices appear in the center ring, with related ministry areas in the second ring, and examples of specific actions in the third ring.
- Journal your responses to the following questions: Which faith practices, ministry areas, or actions are most comfortable for you? Which are you drawn to? Which make you the most wary?
- Write down one action you will take in the coming days to practice your faith.

2. Part of Christian living is listening to God's call, day by day, discerning what it is God is calling you—and all of us together—to be and do here and now. Listening and discernment take time. Take a few moments right now to get comfortable and quiet, and then, just listen.

 Bonus Activity:
Ask the group to brainstorm a list of Jesus' qualities. (For example, Luther mentions patience and humility.) Next to this list, brainstorm ways to practice those qualities in normal, daily life.

 Bonus Activity:
One way to make faith practices a regular part of our lives is to connect them with daily activities. As a large group, make a list of ordinary, daily activities (getting out of bed, having coffee, driving children to school, going to work, paying bills, etc.). Then form several small groups. Have each group choose a different activity from the list and brainstorm ways to connect that activity with a faith practice (for example, praying before getting out of bed, using fair trade coffee, car pooling or using public transportation, setting aside money to give away to church and charities).

 Tip:
Allow adequate time for the listening activity. Dimming the lights a bit and beginning with a brief prayer will help participants to focus.

faith practices wheel

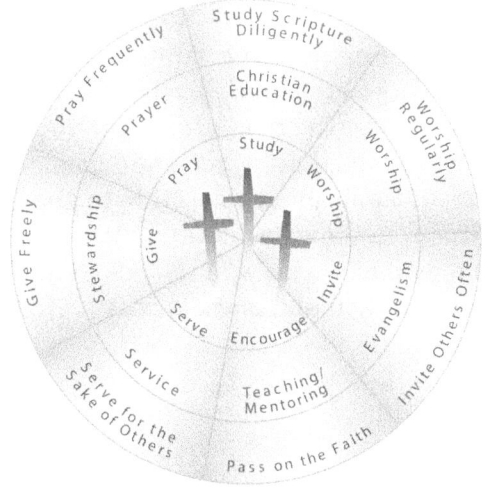

© Evangelical Lutheran Church in America.

SESSION FIVE

 Tip:
Note among the group that your next meeting will be the final session in this study. The group may want to plan a shared meal or some other special activity to mark your time together and acknowledge its ending. If your group chooses to continue meeting or to start a new group after this study is completed, consider using another Book of Faith Bible study.

Wrap-up

1. If there are any questions to explore further, write them on chart paper or a whiteboard. Ask for volunteers to do further research to share with the group at the next session.

2. Ask members to quickly respond to this question: What does it mean to say that faith is a way of life?

3. Distribute small pieces of paper—small enough to be folded and carried every day in a wallet. Ask each participant to write on the piece of paper one faith activity to practice.

Pray

Jesus, be with us on life's paths. Shine your light when we are lost. Walk beside us when we are discouraged. Lift us up when we fall. Strengthen us when we are weak. Through your Spirit, give us peace and hope for the journey. Amen.

Extending the Conversation (5 minutes)

Homework

1. Read the next session's Bible text: Hebrews 4:12-13; 5:11—6:12; 10:19-29.

2. Faith is *embodied*. Tomorrow morning when you wake up, stretch your body to increase your flexibility and alertness as you start the day. Take a few moments to be aware of your body. What are your strengths and weaknesses? What are your resources and needs?

3. Choose a sport—basketball, walking, bowling, running, or another. What is the goal of the sport—to make a basket, block a shot, reach a destination, knock over the pins, etc.? Close your eyes and see yourself achieving that goal. Now, set a faith goal for the week—for example, to tell someone about your faith, to give of yourself more freely, to be kinder, to show hospitality. Close your eyes again. Use the sports image to visualize yourself achieving your faith goal. Use this image throughout the week.

4. Choose one item of instruction from the session Scripture texts. During this week particularly, practice that discipline. Each day journal about the experience—a brief sentence or as much as you want to write. Another option is to list and practice each of the instructions from the texts in rotation, using one each week as a discipline for learning. Think of these as calisthenics to "exercise" your faith.

Enrichment

1. If you want to read through the entire book of Hebrews during this unit, read the following sections this week.
Day 1: Hebrews 11:1-3
Day 2: Hebrews 11:4-40
Day 3: Hebrews 12:1-13
Day 4: Hebrews 12:14-24
Day 5: Hebrews 12:25-29
Day 6: Hebrews 13:1-6
Day 7: Hebrews 13:7-25

2. Prayer, study, worship, invitation, encouragement, service, and giving are important practices of our faith. To support these faith practices, the ELCA provides a variety of materials for individual or group use. Find out more at http://www2.elca.org/christianeducation/discipleship/faithpractices.html.

3. Christians were deeply and centrally involved in the African-American civil rights movement in the 20th century in the United States. Make arrangements to view *Eyes on the Prize*, a documentary series originally televised in 1990 and since then used widely as an educational tool. The series covers the period 1954 to 1985. The title comes from the folk song "Keep Your Eyes on the Prize," a song about faithful perseverance in the face of adversity.

For Further Reading

Bearing the Cross: Martin Luther King, Jr., and the Southern Christian Leadership Conference by David Garrow (New York: Harper Perennial Modern Classics, 2004).

Practicing Our Faith: A Way of Life for a Searching People, ed. Dorothy C. Bass (San Francisco: Jossey-Bass, 1998).

SESSION FIVE

Looking Ahead

1. Read the next session's Bible text: Hebrews 4:12-13; 5:11—6:12; 10:19-29.

2. Read through the Leader Guide for the next session and mark portions you wish to highlight for the group.

3. Make a checklist of any materials you'll need to do the Bonus Activities.

4. Pray for members of your group during the week.

SESSION SIX

Hebrews 4:12-13; 5:11—6:12; 10:19-29

Leader Session Guide

Focus Statement
In Christ Jesus we have the forgiveness of sins—period—no ifs, ands, or buts. When our faith in that promise fails, we lean on Jesus.

Key Verse
Therefore, my friends, since we have confidence to enter the sanctuary by the blood of Jesus, . . . let us approach with a true heart in full assurance of faith. . . . Let us hold fast to the confession of our hope without wavering, for he who has promised is faithful.
Hebrews 10:19, 22a, 23

Focus Image

© Design Pics/ SuperStock

What If Faith Fails?

Session Preparation

Before You Begin . . .

This is the last session in this study. Think back over the five sessions already completed. Think about each person who has participated. Recall gifts of insight, humor, compassion, and faith that you received or witnessed. Take a moment to rest in preparation for the session. Close your eyes and take a few deep breaths.

Session Instructions

1. Read this Session Guide completely and highlight or underline any portions you wish to emphasize with the group. Note any Bonus Activities you wish to do.

2. If you plan to do any special activities, check to see what materials you'll need, if any.

3. Have extra Bibles on hand in case a member of the group forgets to bring one.

Session Overview

In this session we consider some difficult passages in Hebrews—difficult from the perspective of their theology—the possibility of judgment and being outside God's grace. Martin Luther's understanding of the gospel contrasts sharply with the fearful words of Hebrews. Luther's method of scriptural interpretation sets Hebrews in the context of overarching good news of the gospel.

HISTORICAL CONTEXT

Hebrews is part of a conversation within a Jewish Christian community. The original readers somehow drifted away from the promise of salvation in Jesus Christ, but apparently did not abandon the Jewish Christian community. It seems that they may have reverted to an earlier understanding, putting their faith in ritual practices—their own works—rather than on Jesus as high priest who perfected their salvation.

At some earlier time, the readers had been persecuted—tortured and imprisoned—and their property confiscated. Perhaps members of their community or even family were murdered as well. During that time, they met the hardships together in joyful faith. Now that persecution has ended, the author of Hebrews sees people falling away, having forgotten or abandoned the importance of relying on faith and Jesus Christ in good times as well as bad. In this regard, the situation of the audience may be compared to that of many Christians today, living in relative material comfort free from religious persecution.

References to the high priest and temple practice suggest that Hebrews was written before 70 C.E., when the Jerusalem temple was destroyed, although these institutions still held meaning even after the temple was gone.

Literary Context

The overall tone of the passages for this session combines proclamation of God's justice, faithfulness, and promise with the fearful threat of judgment, fury, and punishment. As Hebrews earlier made comparisons regarding the old covenant and the new covenant, here are comparisons regarding Jesus' wayward followers and those who fled Egypt with Moses. Hebrews argues that its audience, in knowing Jesus, has something better than that generation of people had known. How much worse, then, will be their punishment for turning away from Jesus? Hebrews 6:4-6 and 10:26-30 tell why the author writes with such urgency to these wayward Christians. The author fears they will be destroyed as a worthless field is burned over (Hebrews 6:8). Falling away is holding in contempt and crucifying again the Son of God (Hebrews 6:6). Willfully persisting in sin provokes the prospect of judgment, a consuming fire (Hebrews 10:26-27).

The session Scripture texts are not without encouragement, consolation, and instruction. Despite fears, the author repeatedly exhorts and encourages the audience with confidence in their prospects. God is just and faithful. Readers are told how to live focused on community relationships—by "provoking" one another to love and good deeds, not neglecting to meet together, and encouraging one another. The faithful life is life lived in community with the support of others.

Note the variety of images in these passages, among them sword and body (Hebrews 4:12-13), teaching (Hebrews 5:11-12a), food for infants and the mature (Hebrews 5:12b-14), agriculture (Hebrews 6:7-8), the temple (Hebrews 10:19-21), and the Exodus (Hebrews 10:28-30).

SESSION SIX

LUTHERAN CONTEXT

Martin Luther didn't accept that the letter to the Hebrews ultimately denies **repentance** and restoration: "In both cases [the author] is describing the existing state of affairs, not declaring a change to be impossible" (*Luther's Works* 29:228). If the audience no longer believed in Christ's power, they couldn't repent. If they'd forsaken the church, they couldn't repent because, says Luther, there is no repentance outside the church. Luther argues that Hebrews 6:4-6 and 10:26-28 address the question of whether it's necessary or possible to be baptized more than once (*Luther's Works* 29:181). Since rebaptism doesn't make sense, restoration through rebaptism is impossible. No sacrifice remains for those who willfully persist in sin, therefore, there is no second baptism, no second cross (*Luther's Works* 29:227).

For Luther, God's Word is clear: there is forgiveness for any who have fallen. (Luther cites David, Joseph's brothers, Peter, and all the apostles as people who fell and were restored.) In reaching this conclusion, Luther applies principles of biblical interpretation. First, Jesus Christ, God's love revealed to us, is the lens for reading all Scripture. Second, Scripture interprets Scripture. There is a "**canon** within the canon." Portions of Scripture that more clearly reveal the promise of salvation in Jesus Christ can help us interpret other portions.

DEVOTIONAL CONTEXT

What happens when faith fails? The author of Hebrews was concerned that his audience might stray so far from faith that restoration might not be possible. Out of this concern, the writer voices the possibility of people becoming like unproductive land that is cursed and burned over. Urging them to hold fast, he raises the "fearful prospect of judgment."

The good news is that God's love is unbounded. The promise of forgiveness is God's promise, and God is faithful. When our faith fails, we throw ourselves on God's mercy. Christ completes our faltering faith. Jesus is the pioneer and perfecter of our faith. We have not only faith *in* Jesus to sustain us. We have the faith *of* Jesus to rely on when our faith fails.

Facilitator's Prayer

Dear Jesus, Word of God, speak to us in Scripture. Let the words of each of our mouths witness to your love for us. Thank you for this opportunity. Thank you for these people. Thank you that we come to the completion of our study. In this final session, I pray you give us each a foretaste of the future you have in store. Amen.

Repentance:
In Hebrew, *repentance* is a turning. One has turned away from God; repentance is turning back toward God. In Greek, repentance is a change of mind. In both Hebrew and Greek, repentance is something—like faith—that the whole person does. Repentance is not just words; it's also not just deeds. In repentance we receive forgiveness from God, who waits patiently for us.

Canon:
A canon is a list or collection of texts. The Bible is the canon of Scripture. For most of church history, just what constituted the canon of Scripture was open to debate. In fact, Martin Luther attempted to have several books removed, including Hebrews! In 1546, the Council of Trent established Hebrews and several other books as part of the Bible or canon of Scripture.

SESSION SIX

 Tip:
If this group came together around the study of Hebrews, it will be disbanding unless participants have decided to continue in some other way. Particularly if group members have formed strong bonds with one another, the end to a study such as this can provoke some anxiety. Don't be surprised if people's behavior reflects this anxiety.

 Tip:
Distribute paper crosses for participants to hold as they pray. Or give each participant a small wooden or metal cross as a remembrance not only of baptism, but also of your time together in this study.

 Tip:
Some messages in these passages may be tough to hear. Some participants may express discomfort, if not in words, then in facial expressions, posture, or gestures. If concerns surface, reassure participants that these difficult passages are part of what the session will address.

Gather (10-15 minutes)

Check-in

Invite learners to share completed homework or any new thoughts or insights about the last session. Be ready to give a brief recap of that session if necessary.

Pray

Almighty God, by our baptism into the death and resurrection of your Son Jesus Christ, you turn us from the old life of sin. Grant that we who are reborn to new life in him may live in righteousness and holiness all our days, through your Son, Jesus Christ our Lord. Amen.

Focus Activity

Take a look at the Focus Image for this session. Imagine that the person in the photo is you. What do you see? Whom do you see? Then, change your perspective a bit. Consider this: When God looks at you, what does God see? Whom does God see?

Open Scripture (10-15 minutes)

Ask six volunteers to read aloud, each one taking a portion of the session Scripture texts: Hebrews 4:12-13; 5:11—6:12; 10:19-29.

As a volunteer reads the texts aloud, have participants close their eyes during the reading and pay particular attention to their emotional responses. Then ask for volunteers to share what they experienced.

Read Hebrews 4:12-13; 5:11—6:12; 10:19-29.
- What words, phrases, or images stood out for you?
- What is your emotional response to these passages?
- What questions do you have?

SESSION SIX

Join the Conversation (25-55 minutes)

Historical Context

1. At some earlier time, when the original readers of Hebrews were persecuted, they met hardships in joyful faith. Now, in easier times, they seem to have fallen away, neglecting the importance of relying on faith and Jesus Christ.

- Review the session Scripture texts and note signs that the writer is urging readers to return to and rely on faith and Jesus Christ.

2. Having relatively comfortable lives free of persecution can lead to the temptation to neglect faith. Do you agree or disagree with this? Provide reasons or examples to back up your response.

Literary Context

1. The writer of Hebrews uses the educational theory of ancient Greeks, with its different levels of instruction at different levels of educational maturity. Food imagery was a common way of presenting the different levels of maturity.

- Read Hebrews 5:11-14 and note the difference between food for infants and food for the mature. What would you describe as "milk" when it comes to basic elements of faith and Scripture? What would you describe as "solid food" for those mature in faith? What "food" is appropriate for children and for young adults?

- Discuss what kind of "food" you would say Hebrews provides to readers.

2. The writer uses an agricultural image or metaphor in Hebrews 6:7-8 to describe God and faith.

- Read Hebrews 6:7-8 and identify the agricultural terms.

- Metaphors rarely have a clean, one-to-one correspondence with what they attempt to describe. As well as you can, explain what the agricultural image tells us about God and faith.

Bonus Activity:

Most people have had an experience of falling away from the church or neglecting their faith. For many people this comes during their adolescent or teen years. For others it comes when they leave home for the first time. For still others it comes from disappointment, a hardship, or from the complacency of ease and comfort. Ask participants to form pairs and tell about a time when faith waned and who or what helped them to see the importance of faith again.

Bonus Activity:

The writer of Hebrews describes the original readers' problems as "neglect" (2:3), hardening hearts (3:8), going astray (3:10), turning away (3:12), "hardened by the deceitfulness of sin" (3:13), "rebellion" (3:15), and disobedience (3:18). (The list overlaps considerably. In this context, "hardened by the deceitfulness of sin" probably means falling into sin's false ideas of salvation, in particular, relying on our own works.) Discuss: What words would we use to describe these problems today? Which ones are the biggest issues for us?

Tip:

You may find a quick scan of James Fowler's *Stages of Faith*, included in the For Further Reading section, helpful for this discussion. Fowler developed a theory of stages of faith based on the work of developmental psychologists including Piaget, Erikson, and Kohlberg. Since this work was originally done in 1981, Fowler and others have elaborated on his ideas.

SESSION SIX

Tip:
People belong to denominations and congregations for all sorts of reasons—family history, convenient location, friends, particular ministries, and so on. Be aware of the possibility that not everyone participating in the study—member or not—will hold traditional Lutheran views about the wideness of God's mercy.

Bonus Activity:
Read aloud Hebrews 4:12-13. The word of God knows us better than we know ourselves, and gets to the heart of who we are and what we think and intend. Have the group note the ways the word of God is described in this passage. Read the verses again slowly, and have participants listen with the understanding that the passage is about God's *spoken* word. What insights does this give about the meaning of this passage?

Tip:
Ask for three volunteers to do the role-play and give them a moment or two to prepare. Have the two friends alternate saying something brief from their perspectives to the sinner, who will just listen. Allow a few minutes for the role-play.

Bonus Activity:
Encourage participants to get comfortable and quiet as you dim the lights in the room. Ask them to close their eyes for this visualization: Think about someone you want to forgive but have not been able to forgive. Picture this person in your mind. (Pause here and allow at least 90 seconds for participants to focus.) Now picture Jesus walking in and standing alongside the person. (Pause and allow a few moments for this.) Picture Jesus fully forgiving the person. (Pause, then invite participants to journal about their feelings and reactions to this experience.)

Lutheran Context

1. How is Scripture like a "two-edged sword" (Hebrews 4:12-13)? Some Lutherans understand the two edges to be law (what God asks of us) and gospel (what God does for us).

- Scan Hebrews 4:12-13; 5:11—6:12; and 10:19-29 again. What parts of these texts do you hear as law? What parts do you hear as gospel? How do law and gospel work together here to encourage your faith and point you to Christ?

2. Lutherans emphasize that we are forgiven and saved by God's grace through faith. We rely not on our faith, but on God's faithfulness, shown to us in Christ. The Key Verse for this session puts it this way: "Therefore, my friends, since we have confidence to enter the sanctuary by the blood of Jesus, . . . let us approach with a true heart in full assurance of faith. . . . Let us hold fast to the confession of our hope without wavering, for he who has promised is faithful" (Hebrews 10:19, 22a, 23).

- Role-play a conversation between a sinner and two friends. The two friends have conflicting views on the possibility of forgiveness for the sinner's grievous sin (which shall remain unnamed). One believes the sin is unforgivable, that there is no possibility of repenting and being forgiven. The other friend believes there is nothing outside the bounds of God's grace.

- Describe your reactions to the role-play as the sinner, one of the friends, or an observer.

3. Martin Luther taught that the gospel—the good news of Jesus Christ that by God's grace your sins are forgiven—is known by its content. If something doesn't proclaim the gospel, it doesn't matter who wrote it, even if it was the apostle Paul. Likewise, if something does proclaim the gospel, it doesn't matter who wrote it, even if it was Judas or Herod.

- Luther did not believe the letter to the Hebrews should be included in the canon or accepted list of books in the New Testament. Hold a mock debate on this issue. What are the arguments for including Hebrews? What are the arguments against it?

- Tell about a time when the gospel was proclaimed to you by an unexpected person or in an unexpected way.

SESSION SIX

Devotional Context

1. The promise of forgiveness is God's promise, and God is faithful. When our faith fails, we throw ourselves on God's mercy, knowing that Christ completes our faltering faith. We have not only faith *in* Jesus to sustain us. We have the faith *of* Jesus to rely on when our faith fails. Write a prayer of thanks for God's love, mercy, and faithfulness, and for Jesus the pioneer and perfecter of our faith.

2. In Christ Jesus we have the forgiveness of sins—period—no ifs, ands, or buts. Use the words of confession and forgiveness from the Compline service (the left column on *LBW*, p. 155 or *ELW*, p. 321) to confess and give and receive the assurance of forgiveness.

3. If a good friend asked you what you've learned in this study of Hebrews, what would you say? Write down or journal your response.

Wrap-up

1. Ask: What have been your most important insights or experiences from participating in this study of Hebrews?

2. Ask participants what questions they have as a result of this study. Encourage them to pursue their questions in Bible study, in reading, with a pastor or other teacher, or online.

3. Announce any plans you may have to continue to meet as a group.

Pray

Pray for one another from Hebrews 13:20-21: "Now may the God of peace, who brought back from the dead our Lord Jesus, the great shepherd of the sheep, by the blood of the eternal covenant, make you complete in everything good so that you may do his will, working among us that which is pleasing in his sight, through Jesus Christ, to whom be the glory forever and ever. Amen."

Bonus Activity:

The verb *promise* is from the Latin word *promittere*, meaning "to send forth." Discuss: How do the following definitions of the verb *promise* relate to the promise we have in Jesus Christ?
- To make a commitment to do or not do something
- To give reason for hope or expectations
- To make a prediction or tell what will happen in advance

Tip:

Have participants form pairs. Distribute worship books. Allow enough time for pairs to switch parts, so that each person has the opportunity to read aloud both the words of confession and the assurance of forgiveness.

Bonus Activity:

Play a recording of "There's a Wideness in God's Mercy" (*LBW* 290; *ELW* 587, 588) or have someone sing it to the group. After participants have heard the song once, ask them to stand as they are able and spread out a bit to give one another room. Whether standing or sitting, encourage them to dance or pantomime as the song is played or sung again.

SESSION SIX

Extending the Conversation (5 minutes)

Homework

1. Plan a service of corporate confession and forgiveness with your pastor or worship team. Orders for such a service are included in *LBW* (pp. 293-95) and *ELW* (pp. 238-42).

2. Each evening before you go to sleep, meditate on the words "Jesus Christ is the same yesterday and today and forever" (Hebrews 13:8). Repeat them aloud a few times while you turn out the light.

Enrichment

1. Watch the movie *The Straight Story* (Asymmetrical Productions, 1999), reflecting on perseverance in the journey of faith toward reconciliation.

2. Go online or to the library to learn more about the canon of Scripture—its formation, the controversies about what should or shouldn't be in the Bible, the pros and cons of having a set canon, and what books and texts are not included.

For Further Reading

Stages of Faith: The Psychology of Human Development by James W. Fowler (New York: HarperOne, 1995).

Atonement by Ian McEwan (New York: Anchor, 2002).

www.ingramcontent.com/pod-product-compliance
Lightning Source LLC
Chambersburg PA
CBHW082247300426
44110CB00039B/2464